AF531304

Published by:
Namit Wasan

DISCOVERY PUBLISHING HOUSE PVT. LTD.
4383/4B, Ansari Road, Darya Ganj
New Delhi-110 002 (India)
Phone : +91-11-23279245; 23253475; 43596065
E-mail : discoverybooksindia@gmail.com
discoverypublishinghouse@gmail.com
namitwasan9@gmail.com
web : www.discoverypublishinggroup.com

***Edition:* 2020**

ISBN: 978-81-7141-587-8

Solid Waste Management with Earthworms

Printed at:
Infinity Imaging Systems
Delhi

DEDICATION

To Daadu

(Prof. Mahesh Chandra Chattopadhyaya)

Fikr mat karo pyarey dost Achche hain Shahid ke haal!

—SAA

Beloved Parents

Thiru Venkatesaperumal

Thirumathi Jayalakshmi

—EVR

CONTENTS

FOREWORD

Solid Waste Management with Earthworms is an excellent document for the management of the gigantic problem of biodegradable wastes in a scientific way and producing value added products. In fact, the so called 'waste' has not remained as mere 'waste' now, but it now serves as raw-material to produce compost, which is organic in nature and adds to the fertility and health of the soil. This sector is also important from the point of view of managing large scale waste in cities and towns where facilities of resources recovery systems are simply not available.

I congratulate Prof. S.A. Abbasi and Dr. E.V. Ramasamy for their sustained efforts and hope it will serve the cause of society. Indeed I am happy to note that scientists from academic institutions are sensitive to the problems concerning the poor and the weaker sections of our society.

C. J. Johny

Director and Head,
Science and Society Division
Department of Science and Technology,
Government of India.

PREFACE

Till about 15 years ago one could not think of going for shopping without taking along 2-3 shopping bags or *thelis*. Now this is no longer needed. Every shopkeeper likes to provide to his/her customers a paper bag (if the purchase is small) or a plastic bag (if the purchase is substantial; bigger the value of the purchase larger and sturdier the plastic bag). Even vegetable vendors like to pull out a plastic bag from somewhere under the baskets and pour their merchandise in it before handing it to the customer.

On reaching home we simply take out the contents from the bags and throw the bags in the dustbin... to add to the nation's ever-growing burden of soild waste.

Earlier the meals served in the trains were covered with metallic (and washable) trays. Now at several points the same type of meals (perhaps cooked under even more unhygienic conditions than earlier) are given a cover of shining aluminum foil which is neither washable nor reusable like the good old tray. It just serves the purpose of creating an illusion of hygiene before joining other types of high-brow and low-brow wastes in trash-bins (or worse, get thrown by the roadside).

In myriad other ways we are generating solid wastes and, in the process, encroaching upon and polluting precious land and water.

Before human beings became civilized the only solid waste they generated was in the form of unutilizable portion of their hunts (animal hair and bones), and the nightsoil. With civilization other types of solid wastes began to appear—torn clothes, broken pots, discarded tools ... and so on. As the level of civilization grew so did the quantity as well as the variety of the solid waste. The height of it all (literally!) has been reached in the modern super-consumerist society, especially in countries like USA, where every human being is a veritable 'trash factory'. It has been estimated that every year USA produces so much of solid waste—in the form of used/partly used/unused materials such as paper, plastics, metallic products, containers, and myriad other items of trash—that if the trucks carrying these wastes are arranged bumper to bumper the resulting line will stretch from the earth to the moon! The city of New York alone spews enough trash per year to cover a football field to a height of three miles!

The situation in developing countries like India is not any better; rather it is getting worse as noted earlier. We do not generate as much waste *per capita* as our counterparts in developed countries but this virtue is outweighed by our far bigger population and far lesser land available to dispose the waste we produce. With more than 65% of India's 250 million urban population living in crowded class I towns (having population over one lakh) and 10% of it in the overcrowded metropolitan cities, the situation vis a vis solid waste disposal becomes more and more alarming. As a result our cities and towns are facing the threat of being overrun by garbage and the piled-up waste is threatening our health, environment, and well being. Bangalore is estimated to generate 2000 tons of garbage per day, Bombay twice this amount. The outbreak of plague in Surat a few years ago was the direct result of the unmanageable heaps of solid waste pressing upon the city's land.

The municipalities are the primary institutions which are responsible for solid waste management (SWM) in our country. But, most of the municipalities, barring a few progressive ones, are unable to provide the desirable level of conservancy services because they are besieged with a number of problems:

- Budgetry constraints.
- Lack of proper planning and proper concept of SWM system.
- Deficient institutional arrangement without proper job allocation, division or responsibility, and lack of accountability.

- Lack of properly qualified, experienced, and trained municipal personnel.
- Redundancy of most of the old municipal acts in the present context.
- Inadequacy of regulatory measures to control and sustain SWM system, for example, levy of service charges, revision, and rationalization of municipal taxes, etc.

This being the case it is well-neigh impossible for the municipalties and other governmental agencies to solve India's solid waste problem unless such technology is developed which makes waste treatment economically attractive. Vermicomposting is one of the technologies which have great potential in this context.

Vermicomposting

Vermicomposting is composting aided by earthworms. The principles behind vermicomposting are relatively simple and related to those involved in traditional composting. Certain species of earthworms can consume organic residuals very rapidly and fragment them into much finer particles by passing them through a gizzard, an organ that all earthworms possess. The earthworms derive their nourishment from the micro-organisms that grow upon the organic materials. At the same time, they promote further microbial activity in the residuals so that the fecal material, or "casts" that they produce, is much more fragmented and microbially active than what the earthworms consume. During this process, the important plant nutrients in the organic material—particularly nitrogen, phosphorus, potassium and calcium—are released and converted through microbial action into forms that are much more soluble and available to plants than those in the parent compounds.

The retention time of the waste in the earthworm is short. Worms can digest several times their own weight each day, and large quantities are passed through an average population of earthworms. In the traditional aerobic composting process, the organic materials have to be turned regularly or aerated in some way in order to maintain aerobic conditions. This often may involve extensive engineering to process the residuals as rapidly as possible on a large scale. In vermicomposting, the earthworms—which survive only under aerobic conditions—take over both the roles of turning and maintaining the organics in an aerobic condition, thereby lessening the need for expensive engineering.

The idea of subjecting earthworms as a potential tool for the breaking down of organic residuals and nutrient recycling in the soil stems from a number of vital observations made in the past. A few such observations are mentioned below.

a) Earthworms dominate the soil faunal biomass in many ecosystems. The density of earthworms in few Indian grasslands and pasture soils ranges from 632010 to 7911000 per hectare. Their monthly biomass (yield) ranges from 247 to 3330 kg (wet weight) per hectare. Studies on energetics indicate that they assimilate atleast 13 per cent of the net annual primary production in some grass land sites in India.

In other words the density, biomass and energy consumption of earthworms indicate their importance in most of the terrestrial ecosystems.

b) Earthworms play a crucial role in any natural ecosystem by breaking up organic matter, particularly freshly fallen plant litter, combining it with soil and enhancing microbial activity. Decrease in particle size increases the surface area for microbial action. Earthworms also mix humified material (which are mostly ligno-proteinoid material resulting from the combined activity of micro-organisms and invertebrates like earthworm upon organic matter) into the soil and produce about 10-89 tons (dry weight) of worm casts per hectare per year.

c) By means of mucus production, nephridial excretion, and from their dead tissues, earthworms contribute about 99 to 198 kg of nitrogen to the soil per hectare per year.

d) Yet another important attribute of earthworms in soil conditioning is their ability to lower the C/N ratio of the litter by combustion of carbon during respiration. This is very important because plants cannot assimilate mineral nitrogen unless the C/N ratio is around 20:1 or lesser in the soil. But the C/N ratio of the freshly fallen litter ranges from 38.2:1 to 90.6:1. Observations made by in his studies on vermicomposting reveals that earthworms could lower the C/N ratio of the soil from 22.15:1 to 15.13:1 within 25 days.

These observations from a wide spectrum of studies not only support the idea of utilising earthworms as tools in organic waste decomposition but also confirm Charles Darwin's statement "Worms have played a more important part in the history of the world than most persons would first suppose". Several other scientists echo these words to celebrate the stupendous role earthworms play in the formation, development and maintenance of soil quality for the healthy growth of vegetation and microflora.

No wonder some scientists recognize earthworms as 'the most important animals on earth'.

We hope that this book shall stimulate everyone's interest in earthworms and vermicomposting. We thank Bhavna Mahadeviah, our past student, for her efforts in pioneering earthworm studies in our centre. We thank Dr Sultan Ismail, Vice Principal, The new College, Chennai and a celebrated bioscientist, for several helpful discussions. And we thank Science and Society Division, Department of Science and Technology, Government of India, New Delhi, for sponsoring a major project on vermicomposting to this centre. This book is one of the outcomes of the project.

S.A. Abbasi

E.V. Ramasamy

1

WASTE AND WEALTH

Many fancy names can be given to the attempts one makes for converting a waste to a resource—*cash from trash, dollars from dirt, money from muck, gold from garbage, rupees from rubbish, value from waste* ... etc etc. It sounds exciting, this getting something out of nothing, but it is easier said than done. It is one thing to develop a method of converting any waste to a valuable product on laboratory scale; it is quite another thing to do so *economically and on a large scale*. And to do so without generating secondary environmental problems is an even bigger challenge. No wonder then, that inspite of so much talk about 'waste utilization', very large quantities of wastes still go unutilized. This not only leaves the problems of waste disposal in our hands but also leaves for us the problems caused by such spin offs as mosquitoes, rodents, and plague.

SOLID WASTE

All activities of animals, including humans result in residual materials which are not of immediate use where they originate, and which are released into the three receiving media, namely air, water and land, as waste. (Wilson 1981)

Each person throws out his daily quota of newspapers, garbage, cans, bottles and other waste—large and small—without a second thought. No one seems to care much where the waste goes; as long as it goes away.

Waste, anywhere in the world, is known variously as an annoying headache, an unending problem or more correctly as an evergrowing pile of garbage. But gradually the perception is changing, and waste is now being looked upon as a 'resource', or 'urban ores', which contain recoverable materials and energy.

In nature, such of this waste which is biodegradable is being treated all the time; the waste is converted to useful and/or harmless products by the action of microorganisms, annelids, insects, solar radiation etc. But, in the natural scheme of things there is a certain *quantity* of wastes that can be handled effectively in this manner. When the quantity of wastes exceeds these limits, nature is unable to handle the excess pollution load.

TABLE—1.1

Analysis of physical composition of MSW discharge from three typical Indian cities.

Material	*Percentage of Composition (weight basis)*		
	Kanpur	*Calcutta*	*Nagpur*
Glass	0.5 - 1.5	1.04	0.1 - 1.5
Metal	0.5 - 1.3	0.92	NA*
Coal	5.7 - 8.3	6.7	NA
Ash and earth	57.0 - 64.0	58.9	NA
Stone	7.9 - 11.1	10.2	NA
Bones	0.09 - 0.36	0.25	NA
Hay and straw	6.6 - 8.8	8.98	2.5 - 10.4
Rags	2.4 - 6.8	4.4	3.2 - 7.6
Paper	2.7 - 5.1	3.5	2.0 - 6.8
Leather	0.45 - 1.9	1.3	NA
Plastics	0.15 - 0.45	0.3	0.05 - 1.3
Vegetables	1.2 - 3.4	2.2	0.6 - 13.1
Compostables	15.4 - 23.9	19.7	15.3 - 36.5
Organics	19.8 - 23.3	21.8	25.1 - 47.6
Total refuse collection (tonne/day)	450.0	1100.00	600.00
Per capita refuse generation (kg/day)	0.3	0.57	0.23

NA* Data not available

Industrialised countries, with their obsession for packaging and 'disposables' produce much more solid waste than developing countries due to differing food habits, culture, traditions, and socio-economic aspects. Tables 1.1 and 1.2 shows the physical and chemical compositions respectively of municipal solid wastes generated in three Indian cities. Waste characteristics are found to be a function of the population of the city.

TABLE—1.2

Analysis of chemical characteristics of MSW discharge from three typical Indian cities.

Parameters	*Percentage (Weight Basis)*		
	Kanpur	*Calcutta*	*Nagpur*
Moisture	15.50 - 33.1	41.10	8.8 -33.5
Carbon	11.50 - 13.5	19.50	NA*
Nitrogen as N	0.44 - 0.56	0.55	0.51 - 0.74
Potassium as K	0.26 - 0.45	0.40	0.49 - 0.80
Phosphorous as P	0.50 - 0.67	0.57	0.49 - 0.94
C/N ratio	22.20 - 26.7	37.40	NA
PH	8.00 - 8.8	7.30	7.7 - 8.4
Calorific value (kca/kg	800.00	1504.00	1178.00
Density (kg/m^3)		Varies from	330 - 500

* NA Data not available

It has been estimated that in industrialised countries such as USA, as much as 55 million tons of paper, 45 million tons of food and farm-yard wastes, 15 million tons of metal, 13 million tons of glass, and 11 million tons of plastics are generated in households every year. In New York alone—with it's 18 million people—the trash generated per year is large enough to cover a football field to a height of 3 miles! Even in a developing country such as India, the solid waste generated in big cities is enormous. India generates about 210 million tonnes of municipal solid waste each day. The quantum of wastes produced increases at a rate of 1.5% per year.

TABLE—1.3

General source of municipal solid wastes

Source	*Locations where wastes are generated*	*Types of solid wastes*
Residential	Single family and multi-family dwellings, low-, medium-, and high-rise apartments.	Food wastes, rubbish, ashes, special wastes.
Commercial	Stores, restaurants, markets, office buildings, hotels, motels, print shops, auto repair shops, medical facilities & institutions.	Food wastes, rubbish, ashes, demolition and construction wastes, special wastes. Occasionally hazardous wastes.
Open areas	Streets, alleys,parks, vacant lots, playgrounds, beaches highways, recreational areas etc.	Special wastes, rubbish.
Treatment plant sites	Water, wastewater, and industrial treatment processes etc.	Treatment plant wastes, principally composed of residual sludges.

Source : Peavy et al., 1985.

The MSW generated in India contains mainly garbage, with minmal quantities of combustibles like paper; plastics etc. The general source of MSW is given in Table 1.3., Table 1.4 gives a comparative study of the composition of wastes produced in India and in Western countries. India spends about Rs 230 million per year for waste disposal alone which comprises the cost of collection, transportation, and disposal. Despite spending large sum of money on waste disposal, air and water pollution remain unabated in India due to inefficient and improper disposal. Proper disposal of MSW can not only give a high return on investment but also result in a hygienic atmosphere. Bangalore with a population of 4.1 million (as per 1991 census) produces 2000 tons of garbage a day. Bombay, generates about 4000 tons of garbage daily, from its 10 million population. But in developing countries like India, the waste thus generated is largely organic and biodegradable in nature. The common methods of disposing of municipal wastes are :

(a) dumping the wastes in low-lying land;

(b) landfilling;

(c) incineration;

(d) anaerobic digestion;

(e) composting.

Each of these methods have their own niche and limitations, which are described in Chapter 5.

TABLE—1.4
Comparative study of waste production in India and developed countries.

Item	*India*	*UK*	*USA*	*Switzerland*	*Japan*
Per capita MSW generated (kg/day)	0.3 - 0.6	0.82	2.5	0.6	NA
Garbage*	31 - 67	13.00	5.0	14.5	36.9
Paper*	0.25 - 8.75	50.00	54.5	33.5	24.8
Glass*	0.07 - 1.0	6.00	9.1	8.5	3.3
Rags*	0.3 - 7.3	3.00	2.6	3.0	3.6
Plastics*	0.15 - 0.7	1.00	1.7	2.0	2.2
Carbon/nitrogen ratio	25 - 40	44.00	50.0	40.9	NA
Density (kg/m3)	250 -500	128.00	NA	NA	NA

NA - Not available
* Percentage of total weight

Composting of organic wastes has been practised for a long time. Wherein biodegradable materials undergo decomposition and the end product is a material rich in nutrients, called as organic manure or farmyard manure. Decomposition is the natural process of biological degradation and composting is the process of sanitary disposal and reclamation of organic material is termed as composting (Dash and Senapati, 1985).

The role of earthworms in the decomposer system has been gaining importance and the utilization of earthworms in the composting process has met with fair success. It has been said that the lowly earthworm is the most important animal (Abassi 1989). The importance of the earthworm has been stressed upon since Darwin's time. Charles Darwin (1881) in his book "The Formation of Vegetable Mould through the Action of Worms", opined that "earthworms have played a most important part in the history of the world".

Infact, the term vermicomposting is used to describe the bioconversion of organic waste materials through earthwormic consumption (Senapati and Dash 1984). Vermitechnology is the application of earthworms in

(i) producing useful products like vermifertilizer, worm tissue for animal feed etc., for protein supplement.

(ii) monitoring of the environment for soil fertility, organic contents, heavy metal, non-biodegradable toxic material pollution and

(iii) maintenance of environmental quality (Senapati, 1993). There are mainly two approaches of vermitechnology, one is the process of vermicomposting resulting in the production of organic manure and aiding in waste management. The other is its application in the conservation processes of land or reclamation of waste lands; especially when one talks about organic farming, the former stresses on the importance of the earthworm, with regard to its effects on the fertility of the soil.

This book shall be dealing mainly with earthworm biotechnology with special reference to the vermicomposting process. It will touch upon the earthworms, their ecological classification, their interaction with microfauna and microflora, their role in nutrient cycling, their role in the decomposer sub-system, their role in agriculture, the criteria for the selection of suitable vermicomposting species of earthworms, their culturing techniques, and brief reports of a few case studies where the vermicomposting process has been applied as a tool in dealing with the problem of solid waste and some information on the leading earthworm biotechnologists in India.

Apart from conducting extensive literature survey using computerised databases and primary sources (newspapers, books and journals), we also approached the following organizations to identify experts and units dealing with earthworm biotechnology:

a) all universities in India;

b) all CSIR laboratories;

c) all ICAR laboratories;

d) all ICMR laboratories;

e) IISc and all IITs

f) all NGOs

We then approached the individual experts. Detailed visits to project sites and meetings with experts were conducted. Simultaneously we carried out our own experiments on culturing of earthworms and using them for waste treatment. The outcome of these efforts is presented in the following pages.

2

EARTHWORMS

S. Gajalakshmi @ Suja*

Earthworms are invertebrates belonging to the phylum *Annelida* and class *Oligochaeta.* The classification in phylum *Annelida* is based on the fact that the earthworm is a metamerically segmented worm-like, animal. As the animal is further characterized by the presence of *setae* in the *skin*, arranged individually, it is included in the class *oligochaeta*, which means *few setae.*

Earthworms are long, thread-like, elongated, cylindrical, soft bodied worms with uniform ring like structures all along the length of their body. These bodies consist of segments, arranged in linear series, and outwardly highlighted by circular grooves called *annuli.* Body segmentation is not only an external feature but it exists internally too. At the sides of the body on the ventral surface of each segment are four pairs of short, stubby bristles, or *setae.* The setae provide traction for movement. The setae also enable the worms to cling to their burrows when predators try to pull them out. There is no well-marked head but a *preoral* called *the prostomium* is present. Earthworms have an opening at each of its ends, the opening at the anterior end is the mouth and the one at the posterior is the anus. The body is always kept moist by the secretion of the body

* Ms. S. Gajalakshmi @ Suja, M.Sc., M.Phil is a Junior Scientist with Centre for Pollution Control and Energy Technology.

wall and also by the body fluids that come out at regular intervals from very minute pores in the worms' body surface. Earthworm does not have any specific organ of sight, hearing or olfaction, but special cells exist all along the length of the body to take up these sensory functions.

Earthworm possesses both male and female gonads. It deposit its eggs in a cocoon without the free larval stage. At maturity, it develops a cover-like tissue just behind the anterior segments, called the *clitellum.*

Commonly earthworm is so called because it is almost always terrestrial and burrows into moist-rich soil, emerging at night to explore its surroundings. In damp weather it stays near the surface, often with mouth or anus protruding from the burrow, while during dry weather, it burrows to several feet underground, coils up in a slumber chamber and becomes dormant.

The order to which earthworms belong have families which are aquatic as well as terrestrial, members of seven families that are aquatic and rather small in size are termed *microdriles (Microdrili).* The worms in the other 10 families are mostly terrestrial, comparatively larger, and are called *megadriles (Megadrili).* To this latter group belong the earthworms.

CLASSIFICATION OF EARTHWORMS

Earthworms can be classified on the basis of geographical distribution and ecology.

Classification based on geographical distribution

Earthworms are found in most part of the world with the exception of deserts (where they are rare), areas under constant snow and ice, mountain ranges, areas bereft of soil and vegetation. Such features are natural barriers against the spread or migration of earthworm species, and so are the seas, because most species of earthworms cannot tolerate salt water even for short period or the areas influenced by salt water intrusion.

Some species of earthworms are widely distributed. Michaelsen

(1910) has used the term *peregrine* to describe such species. Such of the species which occur only in specific areas and are not able to spread widely have been termed *endemic.*

The most common and versatile of the peregrine lumbricid species have spread to many areas, especially to geopolitical regions that had been once colonized by European countries. As a result the European species of earthworms have become dominant in several regions and almost eliminated the local species. One such earthworm species of European origin is *Allolobophora caliginosa*, which is now common in such diverse regions of the world as Chile, New Zealand, the United States, South-west Africa, North-west Zealand, North-west India, and Australia. *Megascolecidae* are the ones most widely distributed. This family has 30 genera, of which *Pheretima* is the largest with 14 species. The classification of the megascolecid earthworms has always been more controversial than that of other oligochaete families, and in recent years three new systems of classification have been proposed, those of Omodeo (1958), Gates (1959) and Lee(1959), all of which would replace that of Stephenson (1930). The three systems are given in Table 2.1.

Earthworms of the genus *Pheretima*, which are indigenous to South-west Asia, have also migrated to many tropical, subtropical and even temperate regions. Several peregrine species have their origins in South and Central America, and the West Indies; three of these species are now widely distributed in India. Other peregrine species include *Dichogaster* species *Pontoscolex corethrusus, Eudrilus eugeniae,* and *Microscolex phosphoreus.*

Endemic species characterise certain regions. Vast areas that includes Europe, Asia, north and west of the Himalayas (Palaearctic zone) is characterized by the Lumbricidae. The northern boundary of endemic species of lumbricids is the limit of the ice-age glaciation, and still further north (in an area which includes all but the most southern parts of England and Ireland) usually only peregrine species are found. Probably glaciation exterminated the endemic species in these areas, and they were repopulated by peregrine species when the glaciers retreated. The only other endemic earthworms in the Palaearctic zone are a group which includes the genus *Hormogaster* (Hormogastridae), one species attaining a length of 75 cm (*Hormogaster redii f.gigantes*). Members of this genus are found in Sardinia,

Corsica, Italy, Sicily, southern France and North Africa. The northern part of North America, particularly Canada and Alaska, has no endemic earthworms, probably because of glaciation. The United States has a few endemic species of lumbricids in its eastern region, but most species of this family in North America have been introduced to the continent by man. Some megascolecid earthworms, of the genera *Plutellus* and *Megascolides*, occur west of the Rocky Mountains, while the acanthodrilid genus *Diplocardia* occurs throughout the United States.

Endemic species of the subfamily *Glossoscolecinae* are dominant in the New World south of Mexico, Trinidad and Tobago. In Mexico and most of the West Indies and Central America, the majority of earthworms belong to the genera *Zapotecia, Trigaster, Dichogaster, Acanthodrilus* and *Plutellus*; all of which are megascolecids though some Glossoscolecids also occur. The temperate southern portion of South America is populated by different earthworm fauna, predominantly *Microscolex*.

Three regions of Africa have characteristic species of earthworms; these are the tropical region from the southern border of the Sahara in the North to the tropic of Capricorn in the South; the southern part of the continent including the Cape of Good Hope; and Malagasy and neighbouring islands.

Two groups of earthworms predominate in the tropical area of Africa, the family *Eudrilidae* and a number of species of *Dichogaster (Acanthodrilidae)*. The *Eudrilidae* are endemic but the genus *Dichogaster* also occurs in Central America and the West Indies. Some species of *Ocnerodrilidae* are also found in this region, of which one genus, *Pygmaeodrilus*, is confined to Africa. The southern part of Africa has two groups of endemic worms, the *Microchaetinae*, a subfamily of the *Glossoscolecidae*, and earthworms of the family *Acanthodrilidae*.

East and South-east Asia (including India), Australasia and the Pacific Oceanic Islands are dominated by earthworms of the *Megascolecid* group, with atlea;st ten genera in India and Pakistan, and atleast thirty species of Megascolex and about a dozen species belonging to three other Megascolecid genera in Ceylon.

TABLE—2.1
Three proposed reclassifications of Stephenson's (1930) Megascolecidae

Gates (1959)	*Omodeo (1958)*	*Lee (1959)*
1	2	3
Family MEGASCOLECIDAE Prostates lobular (racemose)	Family MEGASCOLECIDAE Prostates lobular (racemose)	Family MEGASCOLECIDAE as Stephenson (1930)
Family ACANTHODRILIDAE Prostates tubular Calciferous glands not in segment 9 or 9 and 10 Excretory system holonephridial	Family ACANTHODRILIDAE Prostates tubular Subfamily Ocnerodrilinae Calciferous glands in segment 9 or segments 9 and 10	Subfamily Megascolecinae One pair of prostatic pores combined with or in addition to one pair of male pores on segment 18
Family OCTOCHAETIDAE Prostates tubular Calciferous glands not in segment 9 or 9 and 10 Excretory system meronephridial	Subfamily proposed Caliciferous glands absent	Subfamily Acanthodrilinae One pair of prostatic pores on segments 16,17 or 19 or two pairs on segments 17 and 19

Cont.

1	2	3
Family OCNERODRILIDAE Prostates tubular Calciferous glands in segments 9 or 9 and 10	Subfamily proposed Simple calciferous glands in segments 10-13	Tribe Neodrilacae Excretory system holonephridial Nephridiopores in two series alternating in position in succcessive segments
	Subfamily proposed Simple calciferous glands in segments 14-17	
	Subfamily Benhaminae Calciferous glands stalked and laminate	Tribe Acanthodrilacae Excretory system holonephridial with nephridiopores in a single series on each side of the body; or exe-retory system meronephridial

(*adapted from Sims 1969*)

The area that includes South-east Asia, China and Japan is characterized by the Megascolecid genus *Pheretima.* This species is also found extensively in India. There are several other genera of Megascolecids, particularly in the Indonesian islands, and some species of Moniligastrids occur in Burma. Japan has a single endemic lumbricid species. The endemic earthworms of Australasia are *Megascolecids,* including some endemic species of *Pheretima,* although most species of this genus in this area are undoubtedly peregrine.

Earthworms of the family *Acanthodrilidae* which are not found in South-east Asia, occur in Australia, New Caledonia and particularly New Zealand (the genus *Deinodrilus* is confined to New Zealand), and also India and Ceylon. Many Megascolecid and Acanthodrilid genera are found only in Australasia.

A few earthworms (species unknown) have been reported from the South Shetland Islands, in Antarctica.

Classification based on Ecology

Ecological classification of earthworms based on interspecific variations has been attempted by several workers. Evans and Guild (1947) distinguished earthworms into surface dwelling and deep dwelling species. Graff (1953) inferred that a deep pigmented surface living variety generally occurs predominantly in habitats with sufficient organic matter. Byzova (1965) was the first to distinguish surface living smaller worms with high metabolic rate from deep dwelling larger worms with less metabolic rate. Bouche (1977) proposed an ecological classification of earthworms into 3 generalised life forms: (i) Epigeics, (ii) Anecics and (iii) Endogeics. Table 2.2 gives the summary of the characteristics used by Bouche (1977) to distinguish ecologial types of earthworms. It seems epigeics have greater potentiality for degrading organic wastes and endogeics have better capacity of protein conservation whereas anecics remain in between.

Another classification is based on the nature of the diet. A high proportion of raw humus would indicate a predominantly detrivorous diet and that of amorphous humus and mineral material a predominantly geophagous diet (Lee 1985).

Perel (Lee 1985) classified earthworms that feed on plant debris that is only slightly decomposed as humus formers and those that feed on plant debris that is already much decomposed as humus feeders.

The classifications are similar and overlap. For example Bouches' epigeics are similar to Lees' leaf mould species and Perel's humus formers are similar to the detritivores (Lee 1985).

TABLE—2.2

Summary of characteristics used by Bouche (1977) to distinguish ecological type of earthworms

Character	*Ecological type*		
	Epigeics	*Anecics*	*Endogeics*
Body	Small	Moderate	Large
Burrowing muscles	Reduced	Strongly Developed	Developed
Longitudinal contraction	Nil	Developed	Least developed
Hooked chetae	Absent	Present	Absent
Sensitivity to light	Feeble	Moderate	Strong
Mobility	Rapid	Moderate	Feeble
Skin moistering	Developed	Developed	Feeble
Pigmentation	Homochromic	Dorsal and	Absent Anterior
Fecundity	High	Moderate	Limited
Maturation	Rapid	Moderate	Slow
Respiration	High	Modest	Feeble
Survival of adverse	As cocoons	True diapause	By quiescence.

Source : M.C. Dash and B.K. Senapati, 1986

The oligochaetes are especially abundant in those places that are rich in organic matter. They play a major role in the decay of animal and vegetable material, and some species form an integral part of sewage treatment plants. Charles Darwin was so impressed by the role of earthworms in maintaining soil quality thathe wondered whether "there be any other animals which have played so important a part in the history of the world". (Darwin 1881)

DISTRIBUTION AND ECOLOGY

Dispersal

Earthworms seldom leave their locality, except with the onset of adverse conditions like drought or attack by predators.

Earthworms are by no means randomly distributed in soil. The possible factors responsible for variability in horizontal distribution are:

(i) physico-chemical (soil, temperature, moisture, pH, inorganic salts, aeration and texture);
(ii) available food (herbage, leaf litter, dung, consolidated organic matter); and
(iii) reproductive potential and dispersive power of the species.

(i) *Soil acidity*

Earthworms are very sensitive to hydrogen ion concentration. Thus, soil pH sometimes limits the distribution, number and species of earthworms that live in a particular soil.

According to some workers, most species of earthworms prefer soils with a pH of about 7.0. However, *Lumbricus terrestris* occurs even in soil with a pH of 5.4. A few earthworms can be found in soils with pH below 4.3. *Eisenia foetida* has been reported to prefer soils with pH between 7.0 and higher, in contrast certain tropical species of *Megascolex* thrive in acid soils (pH 4.5-4.7). *Bismastos eiseni, Dendrobaena octaedra* and *Dendrobaena rubida* have been considered as acid-tolerant species, and *Allolobophora aliginosa, Allolobophora nocturna, Allolobophora chlorotica, Allolobophora longa* and *Allolobophora rosea* as acid intolerant. Increase in pH from 7.25 to 8.25 was associated with a decrease in the number of earthworms in fourteen Egyptian soils. Soil pH may also influence the number of worms that go into diapause.

It has been reported by several workers that earthworms neutralize soil as it passes through their gut by the secretions of the calciferous glands. This is now doubted and a more probable explanation is that the soil is neutralized by secretions from the intestine, and by the ammonia which is excreted.

(ii) *Soil moisture*

Soil moisture influences earthworm distribution. As a rule, earthworms do not thrive in dry soils and avoid drought either by migrating to lower layers of several feet deep or by entering a state of diapause in which they roll up inside spherical earthern cells lined with mucus. The ability to survive in dry soils raises questions about earthworm's moisture content and the proportion of their body water that they can afford to loose.

The water content of *Allolobophora caliginosa*, *Eisenia foetida* and *Pheretima hupeiensis* varies from 82 to 85% of body weight. Their respective vital limits for desiccation are 63.5, 58.8 and 48.6% loss by body weight due to decrease in water content.

Olson (1928) has reported that the largest numbers of earthworms occur in soils containing between 12 and 30% moisture. The survival of *A.Caliginosa* in relation to soil moisture was investigated by some workers. They reported that in soils with 5-85% gravel and sand, an increase in moisture content from 15 to 34% was usually associated with increase in the number of *A. caliginosa*, but increase in moisture content beyond 34% had no effect.

In a study conducted by Madge(1969), earthworms (*Hyperiodrilus africans*) were placed in moisture gradients; they preferred soil with 12.5-17.2% moisture content. A moisture content of about 23.3% appeared to be optimum for them to produce casts.

Earthworms are much more active in moist soils than dry ones, and during periods of heavy rain, individuals of some species such as *Lumbricus terrestris* come out on to the soil surface at night. Most species of earthworms cannot survive flooding, though a fair number can do so, provided water is aerated. Excess water lowers the pH and this proves fatal to some species of earthworms.

The distribution of some species of earthworms also depends on the difference in their ability to withstand osmotic forces.

(iii) *Soil cover*

Distribution with regard to soils under cover of different herbs, shrubs and trees has been studied. The difference in the ability of different earthworm species to select particular leaves and also their acute chemical sense, also influences their spatial distribution.

(iv) *General soil factors*

The abundance of certain species *Allolobophora caliginosa*, *Lumbricus rubellus* has been correlated with soil temperature, moisture and supply of plant residues.

TEMPERATURE PREFERENCE OF EARTHWORMS

The activity, metabolism, growth, respiration and reproduction of earthworms are all greatly influenced by temperature. Fertility is affected very much by different temperatures; for instance, the numbers of cocoons produced by *A. caliginosa* and certain other lumbricid species quadruple over the range 6-16°C (Evans and Guild-1948).

The growth period from hatching to sexual maturity is also dependent on temperature, for instance, *A. Chlorotica* takes 29-42 weeks to mature in an unheated cellar (Evans and Guild 1948), 17-19 weeks at 15°C (Graff 1953) and 13 weeks at 18°C (Michon, 1954).

Temperature also greatly affects the activity of earthworms and hence their metabolism and respiration. Kollmansperger (1955) found that the number of worms on the soil surface at night is positively correlated with temperature, and reported that the optimum temperature for activity is 10.5°C. Satchell (1967) concluded that the most suitable conditions for the activity of earthworms on the surface are nights when soil temperature do not exceed 10.5°C, and there had been some rain during the previous few days.

Temperature also affects the number of leaves buried by *L.terrestris*, this can be used as an index of earthworm activity.

Earthworms can be killed by extreme temperatures. For instance, it has been suggested that earthworm populations in arable soils in the United States may be destroyed by frost (Hopp, 1947), but in pastures or woodlands it is unlikely that the soil would freeze deep enough to affect populations of most species.

Earthworms may still survive in soil temperatures higher than the lethal temperatures of 26°C for *A.caliginosa* and 25°C for *E.foetida* because they can maintain their body temperatures lower than that of the surroundings by evaporating water from the surface of their bodies (Hogben and Kirk, 1944).

Earthworms tend to migrate away from soil at unsuitable temperatures.

The preferred temperatures for *Pheretima california* and a species of *Alma* are 26-35°C and 24-26°C respectively and the upper lethal temperatures are 37°C and 35°C respectively.

EARTHWORM ACTIVITIES IN THE SOIL SYSTEM

Adaptations of earthworms to live in soils

Compared to other animals, earthworm appear to be very much dependent on external abiotic parameters and their constraints seem to be the relatively poor nutritive resources of the soil system, the difficulties of burrowing into the compact soil structure and the occassionally unfavourable climatic conditions.

Feeding constraints

The choice of a food resource by an animal is obviously determined by its digestive capacity, and the availability and quality of the resources.

Food resources in soils

The main resources are leaf litter, living and dead roots, humic reserves and a few occasional or pulsed resources such as root exudates, leachates and percolates from the canopy. Living or dead micro and macro organisms are also a resource for a number of occassional or obligate predators.

Leaf litter may be considered the best resource for earthworms because it is relatively high in assimiable carbohydrates and low in lignocellulose, and has favourable distributions over time and space. Old litter and, rapidly decomposing litter which soon loses its initially high nutritive value is of lesser quality than fresh litter. However, the litter from a grass savanna from Ivory coast decomposed for 2 weeks in aerobic conditions had a greater food value than the initial fresh material. Later on, the decomposing material becomes increasingly less suitable, and the earthworms ingest more but grew less (Lavelle et al 1980, Zaidi, 1985). Compared to leaf litter, living roots have more water soluble material and a greater lignocellulose content.

Soil organic matter may be considered a poor quality resource for earthworms as it is dispersed in the soil mineral matrix and includes up to 75% large, complex humic molecules which are frequently bound with clay particles (Stout et al 1981). However the endogeic earthworm species feed on it. The mesohumic species ingest the soil of the upper 10-15 cm, indiscriminately taking up both mineral and organic particles. Finally the 'oligohumic' species may feed on the poor organic matter of the deep horizons (30-40 cm) in tropical ecosystems. The presence of chitinases, lipases and proteases strengthens the probability that fungi, bacteria, protozoa and other soil fauna are significant items in the earthworm diet (Cook 1983; Lee 1985). Algae, also may occassionaly be an important component of the diet of earthworms (Piearce 1978).

Digestive system of earthworms

The digestive system of earthworms might well oscillate among a 'direct' non-symbiotic system, an indirect one based on mutualistic relationships with the soil microflora and an intermediate system, the external rumen (Swift et al, 1979).

Indirect Digestion

Elements of the digestion of a few litter-feeding earthworm species especially *Eisenia foetida* have been described. Enzymes such as cellulase, chitinase, lipase and protease have been identified. (Van Gansen 1962, Laverack 1963, Lee 1985).

Rafidison (1982), using an electron-transmission microscope, observed the decomposition of cell-wall residues (cellulolysis), mycelial filaments (proteolysis) and humic polycondensates (enzymatic hydrolysis).

The mutualistic digestive system

Preliminary experiments in geophagous earthworms suggested that these worms had poor enzymatic capacities and only feed on simple organic compounds (Lavelle *et al 1980*). When such compounds are lacking in the soil, ingestion by the earthworm is at the maximum, strong activation of microbial activity is observed in the casts and the content of assimilable carbohydrates in the casts is greater than in the ingested soil. In the anterior part of the gut of *Pontoscolex corethrurus*, water and mucus are added to the soil and the pH becomes neutral (Lavelle *et al* 1983, Barois and Lavelle 1986). This produces a sharp increase in microbial activity which is increased six to eight fold in the posterior gut. Since the original mucus has disappeared after two thirds of the gut has been passed, it is assumed that microorganisms have first grown on this readily assimilable food source and then have become able to digest the complex organic compounds of the soil for the benefit of the worm (Barois and Lavelle 1986, Martin et al 1987).

This mutualistic digestive system is especially efficient in tropical conditions, as the higher temperatures favour a rapid and intense microbial response. At lower temperatures, the activation of soil microflora within the gut decreases rapidly, and at 15°C *Pontoscolex corethrurus* does not grow.

Intermediate system, the external rumen

Earthworms, like many saprotrophic invertebrates, may use the assimilable organic compounds made available by litter and soil microflora. Soil would then constitute an "external rumen" (Swift *et al*-1979), and such earthworm behaviour as keeping dead leaves in their galleries before eating them or reingesting their own faeces, or faeces deposited by other species is a possible manifestation of this.

Adaptation to adverse microclimatic conditions in soils

Water is essential to earthworms which have a cutaneous mode of respiration and must also extract water from the soil they ingest (Barois and Lavelle 1986) inorder to maintain their coelomic hydrostatic pressure at levels that allow locomotion. Temperature is an important determinant of earthworms activitiy, with specific optimal and lethal ranges of values (El-Duweini and Ghabbour 1965), Kaplan et al 1980, Lavelle and Meyer 1983, Pineda and Hernandez 1983).

When soil dries up individuals resist through quiescence, an immediately reversible phase of inactivity or diapause, which is physiologically determined. However, these are not completely efficient means of resistance and the decrease in mortality due to quiscence has been estimated to be only 50% in population of *Millsonia anomala* at Lamto (Lavelle and Meyer 1983).

Vertical migrations

Most soil-dwelling earthworms have marked daily and seasonal vertical movements. In a British pasture soil, Gerard (1967) observed that low temperatures and drought were the main factors determining movements of earthworms towards deeper horizons.

In tropical environments, earthworms move deep into the soil during the dry season to aestivate (Lavelle 1978, Fragoso 1985). A rough simulation of vertical migration of a population of *Millsonia anomala* was obtained in the "Allez-les-vers" model, assuming that daily movements are the algebraic mean of two independent potential movements along the temperature and moisture gradients. In the absence of such stimuli, earthworms tend to return to the soil stratum where feeding conditions are best for them (Lavelle and Meyer 1983).

Cycles of activity

Earthworm populations generallly exhibit a marked diurnal rhythm of acitivity. Satchell (1967) observed two peaks of activity in *Lumbricus terrestris*, one at sunset and the other at dawn. Temperature variations appear to be the main factors in daily oscillations.

Seasonal cycles of activities are mainly determined by the temperature and water regimes in the soil and the availability of food resources. Usually, temperature is the most limiting factor in temperate and cold regions, resource limitations and the occasional drought in summer may also be important regulatory factors.

BEHAVIOUR

Light reactions

Earthworms do not have real eyes. But they have sensory cells with a lens-like structure on the prostomium. Earthworms respond to strong light stimuli if they are suddenly exposed to it after being kept in dark for long. However *Lumbricus terrestris* is photo positive to very weak sources of light and photo negative to strong sources of light. But species such as *Pheretima* are completely photo negative and will react according to the intensity of light.

Earthworms react differently to different wave lengths of light. Experiments are generally studied in red light because it is not stimulating. UV rays are very harmful to earthworms. We can find dead ones after heavy rain for the same reason.

Chemoreception

Earthworms can readily identify different food substances and some species like *Eisenia foetida* exhibits stimulation to various chemicals. This is just to enable the earthworms to select the food, give warning of adverse environmental conditions such as soil acidity and help in mating by locating the mucous secretions of other earthworms.

Earthworms can also detect acids. Acids such as phosphoric, malic, tartaric, citric and oxalic which are found in plant materials, are accepted in low concentrations but not at high ones. All species can withstand only a certain threshold pH for acidity and alkalinity below or above which they can't withstand. It is 4.5 for *Allolobophora longa* and 4.1 for *Lumbricus terrestris*. It is understood as seen in the chemical extraction method for population estimation.

Thigmotactic reactions

It is the response to touch. It is very prominent in earthworms and the tactile receptors are in some special areas of the body. There are three nerves in each segment. When placed on the soil, the worms become restless and immediately they will try to go into a burrow and lie in contact with the soil.

Response to electrical stimuli

When a certain voltage is supplied, the earthworms respond immediately and curve like U with their ends pointing to the cathode.

Burrowing

Earthworms create tunnels through the soil as they move. They first push their anterior portion into a crevice and then bore in by expanding their segments and forcing apart the obstacles. When the soil is very compact, they literally eat their way through. A worm weighing 1/30th of an ounce can shift a stone weighing 2 oz, which is equivalent to a man of 150 lb shifting a load of 4 tonnes. Earthworms can be induced to form burrows in soil between two sheets of glass. Burrows of some species such as *Lumbricus terrestris*, and *Allolobophora nocturna* go down to a depth of 150-240 cm, remaining vertical during most of the descent, but often branching extensively near the surface. Burrows range from 3 to 12 mm in diameter, but it is not certain whether worms increase the size of their burrows, as they grow or make new ones. During very dry days, earthworms can go several feet underground. At the bottom of each burrow, a wide space is formed so that the earthworm may take turn in the burrow. The entrance of the burrow is often covered with the bit of the leaves, faecal matters, and some pebbles to stop the flow of the water and the entry of the centipedes. The burrows are cemented internally by the secretion of the cutaneous glands.

It has been suggested that earthworms leave trails that contain pheromones. Such chemicals may account for the different burrowing activities.

Feeding

Earthworms mainly feed upon the decaying organic matter found in the soil. They also feed on leaf and other plant material obtained on the soil surface. They do not feed to any great extent on the leaf material *in situ*, but first pull it into the mouth of the burrow, to a depth of 2.5-7.5 cm, so forming a plug which may protrude from the burrow. The food is first moistened by an alkaline enzymatic secretion which digests starch, making it easier to tear it into shreds. Leaves may be torn by holding them by the edge between the prostomium and the mouth and pushing the pharynx forward. Alternatively, small portions may be sucked in by first pressing the mouth against the leaf and then withdrawing the pharynx, thus creating suction.

Casting

After passing through the animal, the food emerges as a compact, concentrated mass termed as casting. Some species cast within their burrows and others on the surface. The form of casting may vary from individual pellets (as in *Pheretima posthuma*) to short threads (as in *Perionyx milardi*). In some cases, the worms produce a thick and long winding column which produces a hollow mound about 5 cm long and 2.5 cm wide. (Edwards and Lofty 1972).

Eutyphoenus waltoni, an Indian species, produces casts that look like a twisted coiled tube and the African species *Eudrilus eugeniae* produces casts that take the form of pyramids of very finely divided soil.

Earthworms casts contain more microorganisms, inorganic minerals and organic matter in a form available to plants. Casts also contain enzymes such as proteases, amylases, lipases, cellulases and chitinases, which continue to disintegrate organic matter even after they have been excreted. More details are discussed in Chapter 4.

Locomotion

The earthworm does not have specialised locomotory organs. It has circular muscles that wrap around both the body wall and the digestive tract. It also has longitudinal muscles that run between the anterior and posterior ends in both the body wall and the digestive tract. When the longitudinal muscles contract, they carry the earthworm forward by shortening its body length. When the circular muscles contract, bulges are formed along the length of the earthworm. the interaction of these two sets of muscles can produce a series of wave like movements. Earthworm move at the rate of about 15 cm per minute.

Respiration

As the earthworms are lacking specific respiratory organs, they 'breathe' through the body wall, in other words gaseous exchange takes place. The body wall is thin and is richly supplied with blood. Moreover its surface is kept moist by the suction of epidermic cells and coelomic fluid. The blood carries an oxygen carrier protein, the haemoglobin dissolved in the plasma in which the atmospheric oxygen diffuses into the blood, where it combines with haemoglobin to form oxyhaemoglobin and it is circulated to the tissues, where it splits up into oxygen and haemoglobin. Carbondioxide formed from the tissues diffuses into blood, then it is brought into the skin from where it diffuses outside into the surrounding atmosphere.

Nutrition

Nutrition is a combination of processes by which the earthworm receives material and uses them by which it can survive, grow and repair worn out tissues.

It consists of the following six processes :

i) Ingestion
ii) Digestion
iii) Absorption
iv) Transportation
v) Utilization
vi) Egestion

(i) *Ingestion*

Ingestion is defined as the taking in of food. Earthworms feed on the decaying organic matter found in the soil. Sometimes they also feed on plant and animal matter. Earthworms are omnivorous in nature. The earthworms take the food by averting the buccal cavity. Food and some soil enters and this is drawn into the pharynx by suction. The pharynx muscles help in this movement.

(ii) *Digestion*

The path followed by the food from the pharynx to the anus is through the digestive tract. The various parts of the digestive system are oesophagus, crop, gizzard, stomach, intestine and anus. The food after reaching the pharynx gets mixed; pharynx has two chambers, the dorsal and the ventral.

In the dorsal chamber, food is mixed with saliva, while the ventral chambers open into the oesophagus. From the pharynx, food enters into a narrow oesophagus and a crop where the food is stored for a short time. Now the soil and food enters a muscular gizzard. It is a hard muscular organ with thick muscular fibres. It has an internal columnar epithelium covered with a hard cuticle. The gizzard grinds the food with the help of thick muscles and cuticle. The hard particles in the soil help to grind the soft organic part. After the gizzard it is followed by a short and tubular stomach . Internally it is having the epithelium in folds. The glandular cells of stomach secrete a proteolytic enzyme which helps in digestion. After the stomach, there is the intestine which is very thin walled and is extended upto the last segment. It opens out as anus. Finally the anus is an opening in the last segment, which opens to the outside to egest the faecal matter.

(iii) *Absorption*

Actually the process of digestion takes place upto the intestine and absorption of the digested material takes place in the internal epithelium of the intestine.

(iv) *Transportation*

The absorbed food is carried to the blood stream which is transported to the various parts of the body.

(v) *Utilization*

The amino acids from the food are used to form protoplasm and repair the cells. Fatty acids and glycerol form the fat. Glucose and fat are mainly used for the production of energy.

(vi) *Egestion*

The undigested food is passed out through the anus in little heaps of pellets called vermicastings.

Excretion

Excretion in the earthworm is handled by organs called nephridia which occur in pairs in each segment. The nephridia collect the waste materials from blood and form fluids in the coelom in which the wastes are eliminated through pores on the ventral side.

Circulation

The dorsal blood vessel is found on the dorsal side of the digestive tract and its main function is to collect blood from the body and to force blood towards the head. At segments 7-10, blood from the body enters one of the live pairs of muscular tubes called "hearts" or aortic arches; which pump blood towards the ventral blood vessel, where blood flows towards the posterior end to the skin, to exchange carbon-dioixde for oxygen and to the intestine, to pick up digested food.

Nervous system

The brain of earthworm lies above the anterior end of the pharynx and from this a ventral nerve cord runs on the ventral side of the intestine to the last segment. At each segment it is enlarged to form a small mass of nerve tissue called a ganglion. Although the earthworm has no eyes or ears it responds to both light and sound.

Reproduction

The earthworms are hermaphrodite or monoecious, viz., both male and female sex organs are found in one individual and also protandrous, viz., male sex organs mature earlier than the female. Thus, self-fertilization is not possible, but cross fertilization occurs. The copulation takes place during night or early morning from July to October in rainy seasons in such a way that two worms exchange sperms from their seminal vesicles and then separate. When the eggs are ready, the clitellum secretes a mucous ring in which egg enters it before; begins to move forward and when it does, the sperm stored in the seminal receptacles enter the ring to fertlize the eggs and finally the ring passes over the head of the earthworm, and closes tightly forming a cocoon which bursts to liberate the young ones. Usually, each cocoon contains 1 to 3 fertilized eggs (Zygotes).

Regeneration

It is the regrowth of the body part, which has been lost or injured. As it is observed that if a worm is cut into two parts accidentally, the anterior half will develop a tail, but in the posterior half, the head can be formed only if 4 to 6 anterior segments are removed and a cut part of an earthworm can also be grafted to another worm.

POPULATION ESTIMATION

There are some methods to assess the density of earthworm population and species composition:

Population estimation may be very useful to assess the species diversity and population density of earthworms in any area before harnessing them. Some methods to enable this assessment are:

Hand sorting

It involves digging up soil samples and sorting the earthworms by hand.

Soil washing

In this method, hand sorted samples from poor pasture soils are washed in 2 mm sieve within another 0.5 mm mesh sieve standing in a bowl of water. The sieves are immersed in magnesium sulphate solution with a specific gravity of 1.2 and the worms that float on the surface are collected. Obviously washing is more efficient than hand sorting, and it also recovers cocoons, but washing method takes much longer time.

Chemical method

The first chemical used to estimate earthworm population is mercuric chloride solution (1.7-2.3 lts. of solution containing 15cc $HgCl_2$ in 18.25 lts water). Another chemical used is $KMnO_4$ solution to bring the worms to the soil surface (1.5 g/lt at a rate of 6.8 lt/ m^2). A formalin solution (0.55%) is very effective in bringing earthworms to the surface. This dilute formalin is less toxic to worms.

But the main disadvantage of this method is that it is not possible to recover all species equally efficiently; those species with wide burrows come to the surface more readily than the non-burrowing species.

Electrical method

Earthworms can be made to come up by passing electric current into the soil. One lead of an a.c. mains attached to a copper wire which is attached to a non-conducting handle is inserted into the soil. We can use a voltage of 220-240 v, at 3-5 amps, the strength can be regulated by a variable resistance. The conductivity of the soil depends on its moisture content. Worms usually emerge between 20 cm and 1 mt from the electrodes, but there is some danger that worms close to the electrode may be killed by the current. It is difficult to tell the exact limits of the volume of soil from which earthworms can be recovered.

Sieve method

In this method developed by Mira Madan and Neeta Sharma (1983) at IIT Delhi, solar energy is used for trapping the earthworms. Easily available material is used for the fabrication of the apparatus.

The apparatus consists of simple double walled tin container. The empty space between the container is filled with insulating material. A wire sieve is fixed at the top. The garden soil containing earthworms is placed on the sieve. The entire assembly is kept in sunlight. As the soil gets heated, the earthworm start moving through the sieve into the inner container, which has some sterilized wet soil at the bottom. The earthworms are collected from the inner container after about 30-45 minutes, depending upon the season. Fresh soil is placed on the sieve for further collection. Thus, by repeating this process, one can collect a good number of earthworms and these are further transferred in wooden trays or earthen pots with garden soil mixed with saw dust and organic waste for further culturing or use in agriculture, poultry, fish bait etc.

There are two major difficulties in estimating earthworm populations. Firstly the distribution of earthworms is usually irregular and aggregated (Guild, 1952 a, b; Satchell, 1955 a; Svendsen, 1957 a, b) so that estimates are subject to high errors unless large numbers of samples are taken. Consequently, estimates based on samples of a few square yards and expressed in terms of numbers of earthworms per acre may be misleading. Secondly, although chemical expellents (Eaton & Chandler, 1942; Evans & Guild, 1947), electrical methods (Johnstone - Wallace, 1937; Doeksen, 1950; Satchell, 1955 b), sieving (Wittich, 1952), and hand sorting (Bretscher, 1896, Svendsen, 1955) have been used in sampling, none of the these methods can be relied upon to resource all the earthworms present in the soil, and the efficiency of the recovery is difficult to assess.

USES OF EARTHWORMS

Medicine

Unani system of medicine classifies the earthworm as *Kharateen.* In Unani system it is used both internally and externally, as powerful aphrodisiases.

Earthworm baked and eaten with bread are said to reduce the size of stone in bladder and bring about its expulsion, and when dried and eaten they are reported to cure the yellowness of jaundiced patients. In addition to the above, earthworms are consumed to cure piles, fever and to alleviate impotency. Earthworm ashes have been used as a tooth powder in primitive societies and it has been suggested that earthworms might contain a substance effective in curing rheumatism (Weisbach, 1962). These worms are used in China and Japan in dry form for fever because of their anti-pyretic properties and they are supposed to have also been useful in chronic cough, diphtheria, jaundice and also for facilitating delivery.

Their potential in family planning is now noteworthy as they show spermatocidal properties. The characteristics of spermatocidal effects are: i) rapidly halting the movement of spermatozoa; and ii) during the collection or grouping of spermatozoa into clumps or bunches, resulting in specific agglutination. Eartthworms have been used in test for pregnancy, urine from human females is injected into earthworms subcutaneously and smears are taken from their seminal vesicle, both before and after injection, to assess spermatogenesis. An accuracy of 90% was claimed for this method of pregnancy testing (Hasen bein, 1951).

Besides these pharmacological contribution, earthworms also have potency for being used as anti-inflammatory and fibrinolytic drugs. Anti-inflammatory activity of earthworms had been studied in carrageenan induced oedema and cotton pellet granuloma in rats, the efficiency being similar to that of aspirin on carrageenan induced oedema in rats. A method of testing substances for carcinogenic properties was described by Gersch (1954) who found that henjopyrine (0.5%) dimethyl henjabnthrene (0.5%) and other compounds, when applied to *Lumbricus terrestris* for several weeks, induced tumours.

Feed

Apart from earthworms being used in composting, maintenance of soil fertility and preparation of drugs, they could also be consumed as food either by domestic animals or by human beings.

High protein content (58-71% dry-weight basis) of earthworms could be utilised in intensive pig and poultry farms. Earthworm protein is high in the essential form of aminoacids. The presence of specific nutritive compounds in earthworm tissues include triglycerides, squalene and free fatty acids. More details are explained in chapter 6.

Wastewater treatment

Sewage forms the bulk of wastewater. Treatment of sewage can either be chemical or biological, preceded by pre-treatment to remove solid particles in the form of sludge. The most efficient and cost effective biological methods of treatment include reed bed litter, root bed litter and trickling filter.

Reed bed combines aerobic and anaerobic decompositon in a water saturated substratum and it serves as host for several microbes which oxidise organic matter and reduce phosphates, sulphur and carbon compounds to their elemental form. Thus the efficiency of reed beds in wastewater treatment is due to three basic functions of wetlands—physical treatment of pollutants through sorption in the surface soil and organic litter, utilization and transformation of elements by microorganisms and low energy, and maintenance requirements.

Root bed differs from reed bed or wetland in providing soil as a substratum, and treatment is through physical, chemical and biological processes within the plant-soil-water matrix. Soil acts as a living litter formed by the interaction of soil, vegetal cover and microorganisms, ie., decomposition of organic load occurs due to metabolism of microorganisms and plants and immobilizaton in soil. Oxygen and other root exudates reach the soil saturated with sewage through plant roots. Influx of oxygen allows for existence of aerobic organisms in an otherwise anaerobic medium, hence aerobic and anaerobic decomposition occur. Plants absorb organic matter and heavy metals. A great amount of denitrification and elimination of pathogens is achieved in root bed treatment. Treatment of waste can be enhanced by introduction of earthworms into the root bed and it helps in breaking down of organic compounds into simple particles, and provide nutrients to the plants in a readily available form thus hastening the treatment process.

Trickling filter is another biological method where organic matter is degraded by aerobic microorganisms. However, filter without macro invertebrates produce cloudy non-settleable effluents due to the inability of microbes to flocculate solids. Addition of earthworms result in clearer effluent and cleaner filter with less microbial film.

Sewage sludge can also be treated using earthworms before being used as landfills or manure. Use of earthworms is effective in abating odour, destroying pathogens and reducing total mass of the sludge. A novel concept of wastewater management is the use of compost toilets to conserve water. These systems may be modified to provide for microbial degradation of kitchen wastes and human excreta in an enclosed chamber, the process being enhanced by the addition of earthworms into the compost chambers. Provided with conducive temperature and moisture conditions and constant carbon supply earthworms quickly convert organic wastes into compost of high quality.

EARTHWORMS FOR WATER MANAGEMENT

Earthworms enhance water infiltration

Earthworms, numbering 0.2-1 million per ha make permanent, structurally stable burrows in the soil. These can extend upto 3m in depth and with complex network of burrows allow water infiltration upto 120mm. Hence, inspite of a heavy spill of rain, there is hardly any run-off and soil-erosion, each burrow acting as a micro-dam.

Earthworms act as a bio-pump

Each earthworm-burrow enhances water infiltration and water storage over a considerable depth of soil. Earthworms help to bring this moisture to the upper layer by acting as a bio-pump. They also release the water slowly according to the water requirement of the plant.

The importance of earthworm

Agricultural researchers have shown that introducing large number of earthworms into agricultural land doubles the yield, of wheat, increases the field of grass four times, and multiplies clover yields ten fold. In experiments with millet, lima beans, soya beans and hay, Hopp also proved that the addition of live year earthworms increased yields much more than the addition of dead worms did, showing that it is the action of live earthworms, rather than just the nutrients in dead worms, that enhances soil productivity.

Vegetables like tomato, cabbage, okra, and brinjal, grown on vermicompost have shown promising results, yielding quality vegetables than those grown using chemical fertilisers. Germination and flowering are also found to be much faster in vermicompost applied plots than in ordinary composted or uncomposted ones. This increase may be attributed to the hormonal effect due to microbial action in vermicompost. Ornamental plant exhibit large, healthy leaves. Increased number of leaves per plant and leaf area is due to the effect of ammoniacal nitrogen present in vermicompost.

Green manuring involving the use of nitrogen fixing plants is a popular agronomic practice. As earthworms prefer lower levels of lignin and tannin, green manure plants are recommended to be ploughed in at succulent stage in order to ensure effective release of nutrients and their uptake by the succeeding crop. Vesicular-Arbuscular Mycorrhizae (VAM) are known to enhance the availability of phosphate in the soil and their population increases in the presence of earthworms. This disposal and conservation of VAM in arable soil are facilitated by earthworms and other soil dwellers.

The passage of soil through the earthworms gullet greatly promotes bacterial growth. In particular, actinomycetes, bacteria that create humus, thrive in the presence of earthworms. Through their constant burrowing, mixing and digesting, earthworms significantly improve the composition of the soil, i.e., turn organic waste into fertilizer and garbage into soil nutrients. Soil rich in earthworms remain loose, giving the soil a much better capacity to retain air and water.

The method of farming of bacteria practised by the earthworm automatically promotes aerobic over anaerobic bacteria. Its own insides are already highly aerobic, because of its natural ability to inhale oxygen from the atmosphere in large amounts. Apart from it constant burrowing action allows air to penetrate to a much greater depths.

Earthworm feed only on those bacteria that are lazy or unwanted, while sparing the useful ones and this kind of selective feeding is called 'culling'. In fact, it is by far the most efficient method of population control, because it ensures that the fittest creatures survive, ultimately leading to improvement of the species. Besides, if euilling did not exist, organisms like bacteria would multiply in an entirely unregulated manner.

The earthworms can be employed to maximize the growth of aerobic bacteria for waste processing. To achieve this, earthworms are to be reared or cultured by providing them with proper living conditions, and then feeding them with organic wastes. This technique is known as Vermiculture. The best place to rear earthworms is in the soil itself. When bio-degradable wastes are applied to the soil containing earthworms in the form of a mulch, simple wastes like sugars are consumed directly by the bacteria, nurtured by the earthworm. As for more complex wastes like cellulose, they are first broken down into simpler compounds by enzymes produced by the earthworm, before being fed to the bacteria. The rich reserve of bio-carbon that the waste contains is thus put to productive use as a source of bio-energy for the bacteria. Besides, the predominance of the bacteria grown by the earthworm ensures maximum energy utilisation, because they can release almost twenty times more energy per unit of carbon than anaerobic bacteria. More energy release means more bacterial biomass, which in turn, speeds up waste decompostion to a far higher rate than that possible under anaerobic conditons.

While sugar, protein, starch, cellulose, chitin and other substances are biodegraded by bacteria when aided by earthworms, lignins are rather complex to crack. Lignin gives the plants its structure and it is partially modified by the soil bacteria to form humus. Humus gives the soil its structure and has an enhanced ability to hold water and nutrients. A good humus reservoir is essential for producing a fertile top soil which can boost the plant productivity. Nature takes as much as 200 years to build up a 10 mm layer of humus-rich soil. Given a proper supply of wastes, earthworms can achieve the same result in a single year.

A valuable by-product of waste decompostion by the earthworms is water, which is produced to the extent of 60% of weight of (dry) organic wastes. This water is cleared slowly and transported by earthworms to the root-zone of the plants. Earthworms can soak upto 120 mm rainfall in an hour. Since the peak rainfall rarely exceeds 75 mm per hour, anywhere in the world, earthworm ensure groundwater recharge and prevent run-offs causing soil erosion and flash floods. The 'living soil' produced by the earthworms below the mulch can absorb the atmospheric moisture during the night. The mulch also conserves the soil moisture by preventing evaporation from the soil surface.

Apart from water and humus, a healthy soil must also contain ready supply of the various nutrients needed by plants such as nitrogen, phosphorous, potassium etc which must be converted to forms that plants can assimilate. This is done by various bacteria like nitrogen fixers, phosphorous solubilisers, vitamin, antibiotic and hormone producers etc. The soil fixes atmospheric nitrogen as per the crop's requirements and no excess nitrogen is fixed. Earthworms ensure proper utilisation of bio-carbon to produce balanced nutrition for the plants.

Earthworm also transport minerals and subsoil compounds from deep in the soil. In this process the earthworms often transform these compounds into nutrients that plants can use much more readily. Chemical analysis of earthworm castings shows that they can contain upto two times as much available magnesium, five times as much available nitrogen, seven times as much available phosphorous, and eleven times as much available potassium as the surrounding soil.

Ploughing by earthworms can go down to as much as three meters. It also breaks up the soil into smaller particles, thus significantly enhancing the surface area available for the absorption of moisture and nutrients. In the burrowing process, the soil's porosity also increases allowing more rain water to percolate downwards and recharge the groundwater table. Air too can enter the soil through the burrows, where it acts as an excellent insulator against temperature fluctuations on the soil's surface. Soil entering its mouth is constantly being processed by the inoculation of a mixed bacterial culture, and the grinding of rock particles to the size of a single micron. This processed soil is then excreted through the anus in the form of a manure that is known as "vermicastings". Vermicastings are a highly enriched kind of biofertiliser. Earthworms can thus be used very effectively to restore the fertility of degraded soil and wastelands.

Kitchen/organic wastes can be recylced into enriched vermicompost with the help of earthworms and they feed on these nutrient rich wastes, breaking them down into simple substances facilitating microbial action in the gut and ejecting out castings with high manurial value. The efficiency of vermicompost is due to the presence of several beneficial microbes and growth promoting substances in the vermicasts. Vermicompost exhibits increased cellulolytic and lignolytic activity, electrical conductivity, high amounts of plant nutrients like nitrates, ammonium ions, exchangeable cations like phosphorous and potassium and trace elements in forms quickly absorbable by plants. The strong aggregates of casts increase water holding capacity, infiltration and aeration. The castings of earthworms, which consists largely of digested soil and particles of organic matter, is more chemically neutral than the surrounding soil. So by consuming soil, processing it, and excreting the remainder as castings, sufficient number of earthworms help to keep a field close to the neutral pH. Soil that is excessively acidic or alkaline can inhibit the growth of plants and microbes.

Use of vermicompost as manure has multi-folded benefits: healthy soil with soil organisms, limited external inputs, cost effective farming practices and healthy food. Moreover, problems of leaching and mineralisation of nutrients are reduced. Plants are much healthier, with great degree of resistance to pests and diseases in addition to being fairly tolerant to drought conditions.

Vermicompost, or in general, organic fertilisers are better than chemical fertilizers in economical and ecological aspects. Replacing costly yet deadly chemicals with cheap yet friendly vermicompost will ensure sustainable food production. Organic farming, of which vermicompost is a major package, respects soil as a living media and adheres to the principles of vermicompost—earthworms—mulch - plant interactions in food production.

Application of vermicompost increases the growth, yield, productivity and taste of the product. It also improves soil fertility by providing an amicable soil environment which promotes beneficial soil organisms such as microarthropods, symbiotic fungi and bacteria.

Earthworm castings are structurally stable. Vermicastings do not disintergrate into micro-particles when dry or wet and hence does not cause soil-loss due to wind or water. Vermicastings absorb moisture from the air. Vermicasting being granular and with internal porosity and water-absorption capacity, absorb moisture particularly during night and hold it effectively for releasing it to micro-roots of the vegetation.

Earthworms and pollution control

An obvious way to mitigate the cost of fertilizer is generation of fertilizers at the village level through recycling of wastes. This could not only provide a renewable, supplementary source of nutrients but also help to overcome the pollution problem. The generation of waste materials is increasing proportionately with the growth of human population and increasing pace of industrialisation. Preservation of the quality of the environment is vitally linked with the extent to which wastes can be recycled and utilized.

Earthworms, with their marvellous capability of ingestion, digestion and excretion are nature's most useful converters of wastes.

It can process household garbage, city refuse, sewage sludge and wastes from paper, wool and food industries. It is suggested that the worms along with organic manures can be utilized as an alternative to costly inorganic fertilizers for growing crops. He suggested that earthworms can be utilized for decomposing waste organic biomass and in general can be utilized as waste conditioners.

Thus a promising way for the disposal of biodegradable material present in urban wastes is through 'vermicomposting', which turns the material into 'castings' useful for soil improvement. The use of this compost can help to provide not only an alternative to costly high energy inorganic fertilizers but also maintain sanitation in the countryside. (Sharma and Madan 1983)

3

IMPACT OF EARTHWORMS ON SOIL AND AGRICULTURE

S. Gajalakshmi @ Suja*

VERMICULTURE

Vermiculture involves the earthworm ecosystem including the soil, soil microorganisms, plants as well as pests. This technology harnesses the earthworm ecosystem for bioconversion of nontoxic organic wastes into vermicastings, the sustainable biofertilizer that has extensive application in waste management, sustainable agriculture and wasteland development. It involves:

1. Effective utilization of poultry-processing residues that were being wasted;
2. Effective utilization of municipal solid wastes and sewage;
3. Effective utilization of food-processing residues;
4. Effective utilization of distillery wastewater; and
5. Extensive applications of vermicastings for improving soil quality and agricultural productivity.

* Ms. S. Gajalakshmi @ Suja, M.Sc., M.Phil is a Junior Scientist with Centre for Pollution Control and Energy Technology.

Salient features

1. Earthworms, the soil processing worms, have distinct anatomy, physiology and ecology, as compared to the manure processing worms, popular as the red worms.
2. These worms, farm bacteria, the most diverse and productive bioprocessing agents.
3. They provide balanced plant nutrition and promote plant growth without pests.
4. Litter animals such as red worms, enchytrachid worms (pot worms), flies, ants, cockroaches, rats, mosquitoes, etc are the crisis managers that have a role only when organics are washed and create biofire that produces nitrate or heavy metal toxicity. Earthworms prevent biofire.

EARTHWORMS FOR HEALTHY SOIL

The role of earthworms in maintaining the soil health is in three broad aspects:

(i) physical

(ii) chemical

(iii) biological

Physical aspects

The physical aspect deals with the versatile action of the earthworm in the formation of soil, their effect on soil structure, crop yield and mineralization of nutrients.

The importance of earthworms was first stressed by Charles Darwin (1881) in his book—'*The formation of vegetable mould through the action of worms*'—one of the classics of soil science. His observations on earthworms can be regarded as a milestone in our understanding of soil biology and an enormous contribution to some aspects of the genesis of humus and its role in soils.

Different species of earthworms have different types and extents of mechanical impact on the soil. Some earthworms influence the top soil and some the lower soil layers, all depending upon the ecological type they belong to.

Earthworms and soil formation

Soil is formed by the combined process of physical, chemical and biological breakdown of rocks and plant litter. The mineral parent material, be it bedrock or a transported deposit, undergoes physical, chemical and biological weathering. This gets mixed up with organic material that originates from the dead parts of aerial vegetation and *in situ* decomposition of plant roots.

Physical decomposition involves the progressive breaking down of larger particles into smaller ones. Chemical decomposition results in the degradation of complex molecules into simpler ones. These two events go hand in hand, the physical decomposition exposes a greater surface area of soil particle on which chemical changes can take place. Ultimately, in a fertile soil, the products of organic and mineral decomposition becomes intimately associated as organo-mineral, or clay/humus, complexes. These provide sites for the adsorption of cations, thus preventing their loss, through leaching, from the soil.

Earthworms participate in this soil-forming process in five ways:

* through their influence on soil pH;
* as agents of physical decomposition;
* by promoting humus formation;
* by improving soil texture;
* by enriching the soil.

Influence on soil pH

The pH of the intestinal contents of earthworms is remarkably stable around neutral to slightly alkaline. This can have a profound effect on the overall level of soil pH and so on the course of organic decomposition. In neutral or slightly alkaline conditions bacterial activity is favoured, leading to more complete breakdown of organic compounds, and a mull-type humus.

Physical decomposition

The passage of organic material through the earthworm gut results in the physical decomposition due to the muscular grinding action of gizzard, aided by ingestion of silica granules. This provides considerably enhanced surface area for microbial decomposition.

Humus formation

The process of humus formation is often characterized by the selective breakdown of cellulose. The end product is a complex mixture of various organic acids, amino acids, polyphenols and sugars such as glucose, galactose, mannose, arabinose and xylose. Lignin fibers are present in 'raw' humus and peat but are degraded to polyphenols in well-decomposed humus.

The presence of cellulose in the intestine of the earthworms suggests that these animals may play an active role in humus formation.

Improvement of soil structure

The physical communition of organic particles, the amelioration of soil pH, the enhancement of microbial decomposition activity—all these results of earthworm activity contribute to soil fertility. All these effects are re-inforced by mixing of the soil from different strata in the profile. The burrowing and casting activities of earthworms can affect the porosity, aeration, water dynamics, structural stability and the formation of the soil profile, (Lavelle 1988). Burrowing species are instrumental in the mixing process and they act, in this respect, at two levels. Firstly, by ingesting a mixture of organic and mineral particles, they promote the formation of organo-mineral complexes. These complexes are formed in various ways, notably through the agency of organic and inorganic cements. Electrostatic bonding may also occur between negatively charged organic particles and cations, such as calcium. Organo-mineral 'crumbs' may be formed in this way, and these improve the texture, or tilth, of the soil. Additionally, these complexes incorporate a pool of metallic ions that are held in the soil, and are not lost by leaching. Crumb formation is also promoted by the secretion of a thin, translucent peritrophic membrane by the anterior part of the typhlosole. This provides an envelope within which faecal particles are packaged before being discharged from the body as casts. This discrete packaging of soil material improves soil porosity by increasing the diameter of soil spaces, thereby improving the aeration and drainage qualities—further enhanced by the creation of burrow systems.

Secondly, by casting at the surface, earthworms bring organo-mineral crumbs from the deeper parts of the profile to the surface. Deep-burrowing species may also draw fragments of organic material (sometimes entire leaves!) from the soil surface into their burrows in the mineral soil. This two-way interchange of organic and mineral material prevents the accumulation of a surface layer of acid humus, and promotes the dispersion of finely decomposed mull humus down the profile.

The amount of soil brought to the surface by castings can be of the order of 100 tons per ha per year (10 mm per year) from the earthworm biomass of 1 ton per ha.

Soil enrichment

Earthworms that burrow deeply into the mineral strata and return, periodically to cast faecal material at the soil surface may facilitate the transport of certain elements to the surface litter from deep in the profile. There is abundant evidence that concentrations of exchangeable calcium, sodium, magnesium, potassium and available phosphorous and molybdenum are higher in earthworm casts than in the surrounding soil. This appears to be a general phenomenon for it has been reported from U.S.A, New Zealand, Europe, Africa, India and elsewhere.

In addition to the physical mixing of the soil by burrowing activities, soil enrichment is achieved by speeding up mineralisation of organic matter 2-5 times by the earthworms:

* Earthworm ingestion causes an increase in surface area of the organic wastes
* Ingestion removes senescent bacterial colonies and stimulates new bacterial growth.
* Nitrogenous excretions from the worms enrich the soil formed from organic wastes

* Earthworm burrowing enhances the oxygen penetration
* Mineral nutrients are released through enhanced microbial mineralisation, and
* Earthworm feeding increases the interaction among microflora, improving the flow and exchange of nutrients.
* Earthworms eliminate pathogens in the wastes.
* The earthworm gut microflora outcompete the pathogens
* The earthworms produce bacteriostatic substances.

In addition to nutrients, several valuable compounds are produced through the earthworm-microfloral interaction. These include vitamins (such as B_{12}) and plant growth hormones (such as gibberlins).

It has been estimated that to feed a world population of 2700 million people, 1100 million tonnes of food is required, which works out to a demand of 100 million tonnes of fixed nitrogen. Chemical technology can contribute only 7 million tonnes, legumes 5 million tonnes, and precipitation 10 million tonnes to the world soils, leaving a large deficit. Large quantities of nitrogen are lost as sewage and rubbish. This loss is of the order of 4-5 million tonnes of nitrogen almost equivalent to the quantity added as nitrogenous fertilizers. About 4000 million acres of cultivated land in the world is likely to suffer a loss of atleast 50 million tonnes of nitrogen per year in crop production. These losses can be compensated in permanent agriculture only through natural methods of recuperation. Earthworms can thus perform an important function by providing fertilizers from waste. They have been cultured intensively in breeding farms, from where stocks of particular type are sold.

The species commonly supplied by earthworm farms, namely *Eisenia foetida* being used in manures and compost, cannot survive for long in a field or garden. Thus, the increase in yield is short-lived and mainly due to the decomposition of dead worms.

A given area of land can support only a certain size of worm population. Hence, mere addition of living worms to a soil will not necessarily help unless the worm load is low or worm feed (wastes, straw, etc.,) is added with it. Addition of castings is, however, always beneficial.

Effect of earthworms on soil structure

Earthworms affect the soil structure by ingesting the soil, partially breaking down organic matter, mixing these fractions and ejecting this material as surface or subsurface casts. They also bring subsoil to the surface by burrowing through the soil. During these processes, they thoroughly mix the soil, form water stable aggregates, aerate the soil and improve its water holding capacity.

The presence of sand and other larger solid fractions in worm casts in higher quantities compared to the surrounding soil shows that worms can break down mineral particles to smaller units. The proportion of coarse sand relative to silt and clay in two pastures with a large number of earthworms increased with depth, and it has been suggested that earthworms might be breaking down the coarse sand in the surface soil. Earthworm castings contained more coarse fractions than the parent soil and worms rejected finer particles while feeding.

The major contribution of earthworms seems to be in breaking up organic matter, combining it with soil particles and enhancing microbial activity when humification is well advanced. Nevertheless, earthworms are also important in admixing the humified material into the soil. Earthworms have been shown to accelerate the humification to straw as well as leaf litter.

Earthworms form burrows by literally eating their way through the soil and pushing through crevices. In this way, large quantities of soil from deeper layers are brought to the surface and deposited as casts. The extent of turnover occurring in this way differs greatly with habitat and geographical region. In addition, large quantities which they consume are deposited either as subsurface casts or within burrows; so the total is even greater. Such turnover provides a stone-free layer on this soil surface after a certain period of time.

The beneficial effect of the worms did not seem to be due to the cementation of casts by either calcium carbonate or intestinal mucus, for, it were so, the casts from both arable and grasslands should have been equally stable. Ground up, dried casts from pastures could be moulded by hand when moistened into water stable aggregates, whereas pulverized casts from cultivated land could not be thus reconstituted. Evidently, binding substances were derived from the grass roots during passage through the worm. (Table 3.1)

Basically, there are two forms of surface casts

(a) Ovoidal, or sub-spherical or spherical pellets
(b) paste-like slurries that form generally rounded but less regular shapes.

Composite casts, made up of the basic two types of casts are common. The annual production of the surface casts has been put at 1-5 Kg/m^2, but figures at 20-30 Kg/m^2 have been put. for temperate pastures and African moist savannas (Lavelle, 1988).

Soil aggregates are formed by the adhesion of mineral and organic particles. The shape and physical packing of which influence the aeration, infiltration of water, water holding capacity, surface area,. the availability of sites for nutrient uptake by plants, microbial and fungal activity, movement of microfauna, the proportion of aerobic compared with anaerobic sites and volumes, and through these factors, the fertility of the soil.

TABLE—3.1

Influence of different treatments on stability of worm casts and moulded soil from grassland and arable land.

Treatment	Mean weight of aggregates, 1 mm/50 g soil	
	Grassland	Arableland
Natural worm casts	42.00	6.40
Natural casts ground and moulded into articial casts	39.86	4.14
Worm casts incubated for 17 days	38.44	3.60
Worm casts incubated for 29 days	49.80	4.94
Nature soil	27.22	4.24
Soil ground and moulded into artificial casts	10.84	5.24
Artificial casts incubated for 17 days	41.04	5.20
Artificial casts + 0.5% grass roots	9.20	6.46
Artificial casts + 0.5% grass roots incubated for 17 days	26.64	23.88

Formation of aggregates makes the soil well aerated and drained. These aggregates are mineral granules joined together in such a way that they can resist wetting, erosion or compaction and remain loose when the soil is dry or wet. Most of the workers agree that earthworm casts contain more stable aggregates than the surrounding soil. In an experiment, the percentage of aggregates in soil to which earthworms were added was compared with that in soil without earthworms.

After 3 days, the soil with earthworms had 12% or more large aggregates, whereas the soil without worms contained only 5-9% aggregates. How these aggregates are formed is still not clear. More investigations need to be conducted on this aspect.

The stability of the casts is an important factor which influence the soil structure. The stability of the casts have been put due to polysaccharide gums produced by the bacteria by the soil, as the soil passes through the gut of the earthworm (Dash 1978). The production of the polysaccharide gums is enhanced by the presence of the organic components in the ingested material.

Another possibility of the cause of stability is that the soil particles are cemented by calcium humate which is derived from the interaction of the ingested organic matter and calcite excreted by the earthworm's calciferous glands. Another suggestion is that the aggregate stability is increased by the binding effect of fungal hyphae.

Earthworms improve the aeration of soil by their burrowing activity. They also influence the porosity of soil. Earthworm activity increased the porosity of two soils from 27.5 to 31.6% and 58.8 to 61.8%, four to ten times faster than the soil without earthworms. After 24 hours of free drainage, there was little difference in moisture content, but soil without worms was water-logged, whereas soil with worms was well aerated, with water held as capillary water within larger aggregates. Thus, it is clear that earthworms influence the drainage of water from soil and the moisture holding capacity of soil, which are important factors for growing crops.

Effects of earthworms on crop yield

It has been demonstrated by many workers that earthworms

have beneficial effects on soils leading to increased yields of crops. Some of the effects of earthworms on soil take much time to show perceptible influence on plant growth. There is also the difficulty of distinguishing between the effects of living earthworms on soil conditions and nutrient content, and those due to the addition of nitrogenous compounds from the bodies of dead worms.

Studies have reported pore space increasing by upto 110% after the introduction of earthworms in pasture soils, where earthworms were absent. To elaborate a little, in a study, in southern Sweden, the soil porosity could not be related with earthworm biomass. Here, the ecological type of the earthworms has to be stressed upon, because it is the deep burrowing earthworms, the anecics, that effectively influence the porosity. In the study plot in southern Sweden the earthworm communities were found to be dominated by epigeic or polyhumic endogeics. (Lavelle 1988). The burrows can increase the soil volume from 8 to 30%. Soils with earthworms are reported to drain 4 to 10 times faster than the soils without earthworms. The water holding capacity of soil is said to increase due to the colloidal materials like earthworm mucus, which is an absorbing agent (Senapati and Dash, 1984). The root and shoot growth in direct-drilled barley plants increased significantly with the introduction of deep burrowing earthworms. Earthworms burrows may provide channels for root penetration and also improved root growth because they are lined with more plant available nutrients. The burrows make a way for the infiltration of water along the nutrients to the deeper layers of the soil medium.

Large increases in yields of grass and clover were obtained when the soils were inoculated with earthworms as compared with controls, using unproductive subsoil.

A comparatively new angle is the claim that certain beneficial chemicals are released from the bodies of earthworms which increase crop yields. Such substances have been detected in eight species of lumbricids and two megascolecids; they were secreted into the alimentary tract and voided with the faeces.

Earthworms added to the soil in large numbers doubled the dry matter yield of spring wheat; the yields of grass and clover increased 4 and 10 fold respectively. Surprisingly, there was a reduction in the yield of peas(Van Rhee 1965). The addition of live worms to a garden soil was reported to increase yields of peas and oats by 70%, but the worms had to be added in very large numbers (Kahsnitz, 1922).

The growth of oat seedlings in brown podsol soil that had been treated with *Eisenia foetida* for 8 days with that in the same soil without worms has been compared. The dry matter yield of the oat seedlings was 7-8% greater in the soil with earthworms and the total protein yield was 21% more.

In a series of pot and box experiments, a strong correlation between the number of earthworms and the growth of barley has been demonstrated. Increases in yields were proportional to the number of earthworms added. The addition of straw with earthworms resulted in greater increase in the yield of barley compared to the addition of only worms.

Field experiments in New Zealand showed that the addition of European species of earthworms to sown pastures can increase crop yields. The soils were usually acidic; so lime was added to counteract this and then colonies of about 25 individuals of *A.Caliginosa* were added, 4 years later, around each inoculation point there was a greener and more densely covered area, several meters in diameter. After 8 years, the areas of earthworm activity had spread as far as 100 m from the initial inoculation point(Hamblyn and Dingwall, 1954; Richards, 1955; Stockdill, 1959). There are several other instances of increased yields from addition of earthworms to soils in different parts of New Zealand.

A few studies have been made on the effect of earthworms on the growth of forest trees. There was an increase in the growth of two-year old seedlings of oak (*Quercus rober*) by 26% and of green ash (*Fraxinus pennsylvanica*) by 37%, when live earthworms were added to the pots (Zrasheyski, 1957). Black spruce (*Picea marnana*) seedlings showed significant increase in weight when the earthworms were added to the soil in which they were grown(Marshall, 1972).

Earthworms can be even more important in affecting the growth and yield of crops planted in soil that has not been cultivated. Earthworm population was much higher in soil that was not cultivated and had crops directly drilled with a special split drill. In box experiments, addition of typical field populations of *L.terrestris, A. longa, A. Chlorotica* and *A.Caliginosa* to soil dug out as intact profiles and not cultivated greatly increased the emergence and growth of barley seedlings.

Almost all studies on the influence of earthworms on the yield of crops have been based on the addition of live or dead worms to worm-free soil. Comparative studies, on yields from plots with natural populations and those from which earthworms have been removed, need to be undertaken.

Mineralization of nutrients

The ratio of carbon to nitrogen in organic matter added to soil is very important. Plants cannot assimilate mineral nitrogen unless this ratio is of the order 20:1 or lower. The C:N ratio of freshly fallen litter is much higher than this critical parameter. Succulent leaf material often has low C:N ratio, whereas tougher tree leaves (with a high percentage of resistant constituents such as cellulose and lignin that are unpalatable to earthworms and other litter eating animals) often have high C:N ratios. The C:N ratios of some typical organic waste materials are given in Table 3.2.

TABLE—3.2

Carbon-Nitrogen ratio of some organic residues

Organic residue	C:N ratio
Activated sludge	6
Nightsoil (human excreta)	6-10
Leguminous plants	10-30
Urban compost	15
Raw garbage	25
Farmyard manure	40
Wheat straw	50
Cane trash	60
Paddy straw	100
Sawdust	500
Newspaper	(no nitrogen)

During the process of litter breakdown and decomposition, the C:N ratio of the litter decreases progressively, showing that the nitrogen contained in it is not directly available to living plants until the ratio falls to about 20:1, when nitrogen can be directly taken up by plants. Earthworms feeding on litter gradually lower its C:N ratio as they break down the material during their metabolism. The lowering down of the C:N ratio is achieved mainly through combustion of carbon during respiration. Earthworms increase the quantity of mineralized nitrogen and make it available for plant growth. Their corpses decay rapidly; in a typical experiment, they had disappeared completely from soil after two or three weeks at 12°C. Of the nitrogen added to the soil from the decomposed worm tissue, 25% was in the form of nitrate, 45% as ammonia, about 3% as soluble organic compounds, and the rest 27% unaccounted for, probably consisted of undecomposed remains of setae and cuticle and microbial protein.

The body of a worm contains up to 72% of its dry weight as protein, and it has been calculated that the body of a single dead worm can yield as much as 10 mg of nitrate.

Little is known about the quantity of organic material eaten by earthworms. They consume plenty of plant organic matter that contains large quantities of nitrogen and much of this is returned to the soil in their excreta. It has been estimated that out of the total nitrogen excreted by worms, almost half of it is secreted as mucoproteins by gland cells in the epidermis, and half in the form of ammonia, urea and possibly uric acid and allantoin in fluid urine excreted from the species. *A.Caliginosa* were fed on soil containing finely ground plant litter and their faeces and urine collected, about 60% of the non-available nitrogen ingested by the worm was excreted in forms available to plants. Earthworms in woodlands can consume most of the nitrogen being added with leaf litter, and when it is considered that they are not the only animals using this element for food, it seems that the availability of food is probably the main factor limiting the population of earthworms.

Worm cast production and nitrogen contribution to soil by a tropical earthworm population from a grassland site in Orissa was studied. About 31 tonnes dry weight/acre/year of worm cast was produced by the earthworm population. The ratio of worm cast production was highest during the rainy season and minimum during summer. Worm cast contained 0.47% N compared with 0.35% N in the surrounding soil. Nitrogen production from mucus, dead earthworm tissue and from worm casts totalled 72 kg/acre/year.

Chemical aspect

Effects of earthworm on soil chemistry

The release of nutrients from plant organic matter and their circulation in ecosystem depends to a great extent on the decomposer organism in the soil. Earthworms are considered to be the secondary decomposers. Earthworms play an important role in the initial process of fragmentation of litter (Dash 1978). Edwards and Heath (1963), reviewed by Dash(1978), observed that earthworms consume more oak and beach litter than all the other soil invertiberates taken together.

In a more direct contribution, the nitrogen input by the decay of bodies of dead earthworms, nephridal excretion, mucus secretion and casts has been put at 180 Kg/Ha/year in a tropical grassland in India by Patra (1975). This value is higher than the 100 Kgm/ Ha/year of nitrogen production quoted by Satchell (1967) for temperate regions (Dash 1978).

Even if half of this nitrogen is actually available to the plants, the importance of earthworms cannot be ignored.

Further, Satchell (1967) (Senapati and Dash 1984) suggested of the nitrogen added from the decomposed worm tissue, 25% is in the form of nitrate, 45% as ammonia and 3% as soluble organic compounds and 27% of undecomposed remains of setae, cuticle.

Further, O'Brien and Stout (1978) reviewed by Lavelle (1988) estimated that the annual flux of carbon might have increased from 300 to 1000 Kgm/Ha in New Zealand pasture, with the introduction of earthworms and the mean residence time of organic compounds decreased from 180 to 67 years. It is reported that litter was incorporated deeper into the soil when earthworms were present compared to when the earthworms were absent(Lavelle 1988). It was reported that the entire carbon and nitrogen content of the anecics, *Nicodrilus longus*, might be renewed in 40 days, by Ferrier and

Bouche (1985) (Lavelle 1988) . Barois *et al* (1987), calculated that 30% of N^{15} incorporated by *Pontoscolex corethrurus* had disappeared in one month (Lavelle 1988). Wormcasts and soil from the same neighbourhood have been compared chemically by several workers (Dussersee, 1902; Powers & Bollen, 1935; Lunt & Jacobson, 1944; Stockli, 1949; Ponomareva, 1950; Finck, 1952; Nye, 1955). The results show that casts generally have a higher base-exchange capacity and are richer in some or all of the following; total and exchangeable calcium, exchangeable potassium and manganese; available phosphorous; total exchangeable bases and total organic matter. Since the increase of these materials is derived from the plant remains which the worms ingest, the claim that earthworms increase the supply of plant nutrients cannot be maintained on the basis of comparisons of their faeces with soil samples. Earthworms, described by Powers & Bollen (1935) as colloid mills, may be some extent counteract the process of podzolization by producing colloidal material from the soil and organic matter passing through their intestines.

Soil reactions

Earthworms feed at random on the soil. This led to the conclusion that since their casts are usually more neutral than soil from their vicinity (Salisbury, 1923; Stockli, 1928, 1949; Doterweich, 1933; Finck, 1952; Nye, 1955), earthworm tend to neutralize soil with the secretions of intestine. This action was formally attributed to calcite crystals which are excreted by the calciferous glands of earthworms when calcium in excess of their requirements is present in either the soil (Robertson, 1936; Baltzer, 1955) ingested - plant materials (Puh, 1941, Panomareva, 1948). Ammonia, which terms a large proportion of the nitrogenous matter excreted by earthworms (Cohen and Lewis, 1949) may cause a temporary rise in soil pH.

Soil nitrogen

Since earthworm increase both soil aeration and bacterial populations (Heymons, 1923, Anstett, 1951), it is possible they favour nitrification (Keller, 1983, Ribaudcourt and Combault, 1907, Keup, 1913, Blanck and Giesecke 1924, Stockli 1928, Archangelskii 1929, Land 1931, Puh 1941). Several workers have recorded an increase in nitrate nitrogen in soils in which earthworms were reared (Russell

1910, Blanck and Giesecke 1924, Archangelskii 1929, Lindquist 1941, Hopp and Slater 1949a) but in most of these experiments some of the worms died and the increase could be accounted for by the nitrification of their bodies. This is because of the high protein content of earthworm tissue, (Kollmannsperger 1955, Watson and Smith 1956), which is of 54-72% on dry weight and may field an average of 10 mg of nitrate nitrogen per worm on decomposition (Russell, 1910).

Needhamn (1957) has reported that the measurable quantities of nitrogen were detected in the solid faecal matter of earthworms fed on elm leaves which contained 6.6 mg of nitrogen per gram dry weight. This suggests that earthworms are efficient in metabolizing the nitrogen of plant material. In forest soils the proportion of N and D-amino acid has been found (Wittich, 1952) to increase with improving quality of humus, and there is evidence of an increased—amines—N production in the presence of great earthworm activity.

Biological aspect

Earthworms and agriculture

Earthworms play a crucial role in a) 'tilling' the soil b) orienting its chemical and biological characteristics to suit agriculture c) help in retention of water in the soil, and movement of water through the soil to enhance its availability to plants.

Consumption, turnover, and humification

Earthworms are able to consume very large amount of litter, and the amount they turn over seems to be more dependent on the total amount of suitable organic matter available than on other factors. If physical soil conditions are suitable, the number of worms usually increase until food becomes a limiting factor.

Earthworms pass a mixture of organic and inorganic matter through their guts when feeding or burrowing, and in particular surface-feeding worms, such as *L.terrestris*, consume large amounts of organic matter. The smaller earthworms that feed on litter in woodlands, such as *L.castaneus* and *E.foetida* produce casts that are almost entirely fragmented litter, whereas larger species such as

A.longa and *A.caliginosa* consume a large proportion of soil, and, there is less organic matter in their casts. Lumbricids, in old pasture land at Rothamsted, consumed between 50 to 90 tonnes of oven-dry soil per ha according to calculations by Evans (1948), but this was certainly an underestimate as the sampling method he used was inefficient. When individuals of *A. longa, A. caliginosa* and *L. rubellus* were fed on cowdung in cultures for two years, the average dry weight of dung each individual consumed during this time was 35-40 g, 20-24g and 16-20g respectively (Guild, 1955), and on this basis, the annual consumption of dung in the field by these species, at a population density of 120,000 adults per ha, would be 17-20 tonnes per ha, with a total estimated consumption for the whole population is of about 25-30 tonnes per ha. Immature individuals of *A.caliginosa* consumed dung in culture, at a rate of 80 mg of oven-dried matter per g of fresh weight of worm (Barley, 1959), which was about twice the amount reported by Guild for this species. The amount of dung produced by dairy cattle (6-7.5 tonnes per ha) has been estimated as only one quarter of the amount that a typical earthworm population could consume (Satchell, 1967; Edwards and Lofty 1972).

When the rate of through-put of soil by *Octolasium* sp. in cultures of soil tagged with radiocaesium (^{137}Cs) was calculated, they found that soil passed through the worms' guts at a rate of about 86 mg per day per worm, equivalent to 28.8% of the live weight of the earthworm. This compares well with calculations by Satchell (1967), who multiplied the weight of soil in dissected earthworms by an estimate of how rapidly food passes through their guts, that showed that individuals of *L. terrestris* consumed 100-120 mg or 10-30% of their live body weight per day and individuals of *A. longa*, 20% of their live body weight per day.

In an apple orchard, *L. terrestris* consumed the equivalent of 2,000 kg per ha of leaf litter between leaf fall and the end of February (98.6% of the total leaf fall) (Raw, 1962), and various workers have calculated the amount of different species of leaf litter eaten by earthworms. *L. rubellus* consumed 20.4 mg dry weight of hazel litter per worm (Franz and Leitenberger, 1948), six other species of worms consumed an average 27 mg of alder leaves per g fresh weight of worm (van Rhee, 1963), and *L. terrestris* consumed about 80 mg of elm leaves per g fresh weight of worm (Needham, 1957).

The weight of leaves that falls annually in woodlands has been estimated as varying from as little as 0.5 tonnes per ha per year in alpine and arctic forests, to 2.5-3.5 tonnes per ha per year in stable temperate forests, and as much as 5.5-15 tonnes per ha per year in tropical forests (Bray and Gorham, 1964), Satchell (1967) calculated that if a temperate deciduous woodland has a leaf fall of 3 tonnes per ha per year and if earthworms consume 27 mg per g leaf litter per day, which is a reasonable average expectation, then they would consume the annual leaf fall in about three months. Madge (1966) calculated that in tropical forests in Nigeria, the litter fall was three or four times as much as in a temperate forest, and suggested that earthworms were the most important animals in fragmenting and incorporating it.

Even when organic material such as dung or litter is freely available to earthworms, many species also ingest large quantities of mineral soil. When individuals of *A. caliginosa* had unlimited quantities of litter available, they still ingested 200-300 mg of soil per gram of body weight per day, and the ingested mineral soil passed through the gut in about twenty hours (Barley, 1961).

The final process in organic matter decomposition is known as humification, and this is basically the breaking down of large particles of organic matter into simple soluble forms of N,P,K and other mineral compounds that can enter the soil to provide the nourishments for growing plant. Only about one-quarter of the fresh organic matter becomes converted to humus. Much of the humification process is due to smaller soil organisms, such as microorganisms, mites, springtails and other arthropods, but is also accelerated by the passage of the organic material through the guts of earthworms feeding on decomposed organic matter together with mineral soil. Probably some of the final stages of humification are due to the intestinal microflora in the earthworms'gut, because most of the evidence indicates that the chemical processes of humification are caused more by the microflora than by the fauna. The full role of earthworms in the decomposition of the more resistant organic remains is still not clear and needs more study. The major contribution of earthworms seem to be in breaking up of organic matter, combining it with soil particles and enhancing microbial activity when humification is well advanced. Nevertheless, earthworms are also important in mixing the humified material into the soil.

Organic matter and nutrient cycling

The consequence of earthworm activities on the cycling of organic matter and nutrients may be divided into dust effects, at the scale of the gut transit of a single individual or population, and indirect effects, at the scale of the whole soil system (i.e. strategies of nutrient cycling).

Removal of blockages

By conditioning their environment and providing readily assimilable organic matter, earthworms greatly influence microbial activity.

In temperate forest, esters, phenol protein complexes constitute a difficult obstacle that only a few decomposers can efficiently overturn (Toutain 1981). At a further stage of the decomposition process, organic matter is largely composed of highly condensed humic molecules which are not very amenable to microbial decompositon and constitute the "slow" and passive carbon (Parton et.al. 1984).

Earthworms overcome both barriers, when they activate the free soil microflora by creating suitable environmental conditions and by providing readily assimilable energy substrates.

It accelerates the organic-matter cycle by increasing both mineralisation and humification. This results in a decrease in the mean residence time of carbon in the soil, better mixing of organic compounds throughout the soil profile and, at times, a decrease in organic-matter accumulation in the soil (Stout and Goh 1980).

Earthworms farm bacteria

Microbial activity is important in the primary breakdown of the complex substances. The presence of large numbers of bacteria of different species in the earthworm gut plays a major role in the breakdown of complex substances. Earthworms themselves are thus secondary decomposers.

The microbial breakdown of complex substances, enables soil macrofauna to use the intermediate metabolic products and degradation products (Dash and Senapati,1985). The crushing action of the earthworms resulting in the physical breakup of the material, results in the increase of the surface area for further microbial action. In all species of earthworms, the total number of plant material pieces were minimum in the foregut region and number gradually increased in the midgut and hind gut regions and in fresh casts. This indicates that the plant materials were subjected to fragmentation. The total surface area of plant material in different regions of the gut of *Drawida calebi* and *Drawida willsi* remained more or less the same, whereas in *Octochaetona surensis* and *Lampito mauritii*, these exhibited a decreasing trend. Maybe in the gut of *O.surensis* and *L. mauritii*, the plant materials were subjected to decomposition. It is suggested that microbial decomposition processes are speeded up, if simple nitrogenous compounds are added, the waste products of earthworms thus, may stimulate the decomposition process (Edwards and Lofty 1972). Also, the grazing activity of earthworms over the microflora may help in the prevention of the formation of aged and stagnant populations of the microbes. This grazing activity by the earthworms also seems to help in dispersion of some of the microbes. It was found that the rate of spread of fungi was much faster in the presence of earthworms (Lee, 1985).

The microbes themselves seem to be a part of the earthworm diet, Satchell (1963) suggested, on considering the nitrogen needed for tissue production and that which is ingested, that sufficient nitrogen could be ingested, if the worms were feeding on the microbial protein among other proteinous sources as well. More evidence to support the significance of microbes in the earthworm diet comes from the work of Hansen and Cyochanska, reported by Lee(1985) wherein a susbstantial proportion of the fatty acids identified were those characteristically synthesised by microbes.

As a direct effect of feeding on microbes, Hartenstein (1981) said in the course of feeding on anaerobes, aerobic conditions are produced, thus obvitiating environmental conditions for these microbes which are causative agents of malodours.

Further the consumers of dead organic matter are the living associates of the debris, not on the debris itself, which may be merely as suitable vehicle to transport the micro-organism into the gut.

TABLE—3.3

Microfungi isolated from the surrounding soil, different regions of the gut contents and freshly laid cast in four species of earthworms

FG = Foregut, MG = Midgut, HG = Hindgut, C = Cast, + isolated, - not isolated

Microfungi	Soil	Earthworm Species															
		D.calebi				O.surensis				L.mauritii				D.willsi			
		FG	MG	HG	C	FG	MG	HG	C	FG	MG	HG	C	FG	MG	HG	C
1	2	3	4	5	6	7	8	9	10	11	12	13	14	15	16	17	18
Aspergillus flavus Link	+	+	+	+	+	+	+	+	+	+	+	+	+	+	+	+	+
Aspergillus fumigatus Fresenius	+	+	+	+	+	+	+	+	+	+	+	+	+	+	+	+	+
Aspergillus niger Van Tieghem	+	+	+	+	+	+	+	+	+	+	+	+	+	+	+	+	+
Aspergillus terreus Thom	+	+	+	+	+	+	+	+	+	+	+	+	+	+	+	+	+
Penicillium sp. A	+	+	+	+	+	+	+	+	+	+	+	+	+	+	+	+	+
Penicillium sp.B	+	+	+	+	+	-	-	-	-	-	-	-	-	-	-	-	-
Thielavia terricola (Gilman and Abbott Emmons)	+	+	+	+	+	+	+	+	+	+	+	+	+	+	+	+	+
Trichoderma sp.	+	+	+	-	-	+	+	+	-	+	+	+	-	+	+	+	-
Botryotrichum sp.	+		-	-	+	+	+	+	-	-	-	-	+	+	+	+	+

(Cont.)...

1	2	3	4	5	6	7	8	9	10	11	12	13	14	15	16	17	18
Fusarium sp.	+	+	-	-	-	+	+	+	-	+	+	-	-	+	+	-	
Rhizopus nigricans Ehrenberg	+	+	-	-	-	-	-	-	-	+	+	-	-	+	+	+	-
Curvularia sp.	+	+	-	-	-	+	+	-	-	-	-	-	-	+	+	-	-
Chaetomium sp.	+	-	-	-	-	+	-	-	-	-	-	-	-	+	+	-	-
Neocosmospora vasinfecta E.F. Smith	+	+	+	+	+	-	-	-	-	+	+	+	+	-	-	-	-
Cladosporium sp.	+	-	-	-	-	-	-	-	-	+	+	-	-	-	-	-	-
Syncephalastrum racemosum (Cohn) Schroeter	+	+	+	-	-	-	-	-	-	+	+	-	-	-	-	-	-
Actinomucor sp.	+	-	-	-	-	-	-	-	-	+	-	-	-	-	-	-	-
Mucor sp.	+	-	-	-	-	-	-	-	-	-	-	-	-	-	-	-	-
Helminthosporium sp.	+	+	-	-	-	-	-	-	-	-	-	-	-	-	-	-	-
Nigrospora sphaerica (Saccardo) Mason	+	+	-	-	-	-	-	-	-	-	-	-	-	-	-	-	-
Cunninghamella sp.	+	+	+	-	-	-	-	-	-	-	-	-	-	-	-	-	-
Total	21	16	11	8	7	11	10	9	7	13	12	8	7	12	12	9	7

Earthworms such as *Eisenia foetida* are known to contain bacterial enzymes. This property was tried out on viruses like the Cow Pea Mosaic Virus (CPMV) and Tobacco Mosaic Virus (TMV), these viruses are non-enveloped viruses similar to the pathogenic non-enveloped viruses like poliovirus. So, the effects on TMV and CPMV can be viewed as a model on other non-enveloped viruses. Viral antigenicity and infectivity was found to decrease following passage through the earthworms and elimination in castings. There is the possibility of application of earthworms in decreasing the potential pathogenecity of the micro organisms, for example when sewage is applied onto land, earthworms can be inoculated into the land, to graze on the sewage along with its microbial components.

Table 3.3 shows the Microfungi isolated from the surrounding soil, different region of the gut contents and freshly laid cast in 4 species of arthworms. On the basis of the presence and absence of the microfungi in the different regions of the gut, it is concluded that there exist the gradient with regard to the digestive capability of different regions of the gut of the earthworms for the use of microfungi as food. The annual ingestion amounts of fungal material was calculated to be 0.878 gms for *D. calebi*, 5.818 gms for *O.surensis*, 5.13 gms for *L.mauritii*, 0.597 gms for*D. willsi*Even though *D.willsi* ingests less, its assimilation efficiency.

Even though *D.willsi* ingests less, its assimilation efficiency is the highest and as such it is of relative importance as microfungal grazer.

Bacteria are the most voracious consumers of waste organics. While 1,000 kg biomass of fungi may consume 2,000 kg waste organics per day, the same biomass of bacteria may consume about 20,000 kg waste organics per day. 1,000 kg biomass of earthworms consume about 500 kg of bacteria and other microbes as their food. 100 kg of waste organics can produce about 10kg bacteria which, in turn can produce about 1 kg earthworms.

Earthworms harness the beneficial soil bacteria to produce various inputs for the plants. It culls the undesirable and excess bacteria and have them as their food. Such culling ensures that bacteria maintain their high growth rates in the limited resource of nutrients and space. This, in turn, results in speedy and effective bioconversion of waste organics into resources.

Earthworm speedup bioprocessing of waste organics due to the bacteria farmed by them. Without bacteria, they would consume only half of their body weight of waste organics per day. By feeding the waste organics to the bacteria, earthworms increase their own consumption to 0.5x20 = 10 times their body weight per day—twenty times higher than that possible without the food-chain effect.

One can convert wastes into resources by harnessing the bacteria as the prime processors and earthworms as bio-managers.

Fixation of nutrients by earthworms

Soil improvement is very important to make use of even in the less productive land to increase food production. Mineral aggregates are more stable in the presence of organic particles and this is because the deficiency of the organic carbon hinders the retention of N,S and P in soils and their loss affects soil fertility.

The selectively fed organic matter undergoes physical breakdown more than chemical in the gut of worms. This provides larger surface area for establishment of microbial populations which actually enhance the decomposition. The worm worked sugarcane trash and other agricultural stubbles had higher metabolic rate, increased cellulolytic and lignolytic activity than controls without worms. An increase in electrical conductivity in cast than in surrounding soil attributes to enhanced mineralisation. The application of vermicompost to paddy field resulted in increase in the population of beneficial microbes like N fixers and of Mycorrhizae, the symbiotic fungal population with simple application over the control plots.

Slightly higher level of carbon and nitrogen ratio in the cast is probably due to the inability of the worms to digest the material they ingest and this is brought down after the action of the microbes on this enriched medium. With respect to other exchangable cations and phosphorous and potassium, an increase in cast than in the surrounding soil was observed.

SUSTAINABLE AGRICULTURE

Sustainable agriculture is one in which the goal is permanently Achieved through the utilisation of renewable resources.

Basic elements of sustainable agriculture are conservation of energy, soil and water. Moreover it avoids the use of synthetic fertilisers, pesticides, growth regulators and live-stock feed additives. To the maximum extent feasible, this system relies upon:

a. efficient recycling of non residues, animal manures, green manures, off-farm organic wastes—reducing their pollution potential, simultaneously

b. minimum mechanical cultivation, to maintain soil productivity and tilth

c. mineral bearing rocks to supply plant nutrients

d. increase in the pest-resistance through balanced nutrition of the plants

e. biological pest control

f. crop rotation

g. mixed cropping

It is possible to effect a quick change-over to sustainable agriculture by harnessing vermiculture biotechnology to the soil.

Good earthworm population is a measure of soil productivity. Hence, establishing an earthworm population of 0.2-1.0 million per hectare within a short period of three months is the key to a quick change-over without a significant loss of yield. Difficult considerations in this regard, are:

1. Worms should be of deep burrowing type, they possess digging muscles enabling them protection from harsh field conditions.

2. Burrowing worms show high mortality when shifted from one place to another due to environmental shock. Hence they should be hatched in the new environment, from vermicastings containing worm cocoons and beneficial soil microflora.

3. The package should be simple and cost effective to the farmers. The package consists of:

Apply first, a layer of vermicastings at the rate of 5 tons per ha, only in areas where sufficient moisture is present, like basins below trees, below drippers or in furrows. Feeding earthworms with fresh animal dung in 20 mm layer below the mulch is possible. Watering every 15-20 days is essential as the mulch reduces mositure loss from the soil.

Organic materials like weeds, agricultural residues, city wastes or food-processing wastes can be used for mulching. Worms hatch out within a month, start processing the organic mulch and, produce vermicastings. No further doses are ideally required to be added. Thus it makes the package cost-effective to the farmers.

Soil Biotechnology

Worms build up density of beneficial bacteria and actinomycetes 1,000 times inside their guts by providing optimum conditions of temperature, moisture, aeration and pH, which also assimilate, some of the microorganisms as their food. They produce several enzymes which split complex polymers in wastes into simple molecules which are further utilised by the soil micro-organisms.

Hence, more the microbial biomass in the soil, more will be the worm biomass which can be supported by the soil. Higher the worm activity, better the microbial action, leading to soil productivity. Earthworms enrich the soil with oxygen, encouraging aerobic microorganisms which perform several important functions like:

> nitrogen - fixation, nitrification, production of enzymes, antibiotics, growth-hormones and also destroy pathogens due to pest infection, other troublesome organisms like nematodes are reduced by worm action.

Benefits of sustainable agriculture

To Farmers

i) low cost of production

ii) enhancement of soil fertility

iii) more yield with lesser irrigation

iv) keeping qualities, leaves notoxic residues, fetching a higher price

To Environment

i) wastes create no pollution
ii) more groundwater recharge and lesser depletion of groundwater
iii) soil salinization reduced, lesser soil erosion.

To National Economy

i) Lesser pollution from agro-chemicals
ii) Lesser imports, saving valuable foreign exchange
iii) More export of agricultural produce with lower pesticide residues

Earthworms: Natural Bioreactors

Earthworms convert the soil into a bioreactor complex by changing the soil characteristics suitable for making it an ideal immobilised - bed bioreactor. Soil is processed by earthworms to produce high specific surface areas, enabling the soil to immobilise a high biomass of bacteria in a given volume. Since one is interested in hastening up the decomposition process and since microbes are considered as primary decomposers and the earthworms as secondary decomposers, their interrelationship is important.

Lavelle (1988) suggested that the digestive systems of earthworms varies from a " direct" non-symbiotic system to an indirect one based on mutualistic relationship with soil microorganisms. In direct digestion, it is suggested that the earthworms can digest the complex organic compounds with high C/N ratios using enzymes like cellulase, chitinase, lipase, protease. But it is unclear whether the digestive enzymes have been produced by the earthworm or by resident microflora. Some of the enzymes in earthworm and their activity is shown in Tables 3.4 and 3.5. Senapati and Dash (1984) have suggested that the question of whether the enzymes like cellulase or chitinase present in the various earthworm species are produced by the gut microorganisms or by the earthworms themselves may not be important from the ecological point of view as long as the possible association between earthworms and substrate degradation is constant.

In the mutualistic digestive system the micro- organisms in the gut of the earthworm aids in assimilation of nutrients. Taking an example of *Pontoscolex corethrurus*, water and mucus are added to the soil ingested, bringing the pH near neutral, this produces an increase in microbial activity. It is assumed that the mucus serves as a readily assimiable food source for the microbes, later these microbes work upon the more complex compounds present in the ingested material, benefiting the earthworms. It is suggested that the intestinal mucus of earthworms is a chemical mediator in the activity of microbes. The intermediate system suggested is that the soil as an external rumen, providing and making available assimiable organic matter in the form of litter and soil microflora.

TABLE 3.4
Gut enzymes of earthworms

Earthworm species	Gut enzymes				
	Amylase	Cellulase	Chitinase	Proteas	Urease
Dichogaster bolaui	+	+	-	+	+
Drawida calebi	+	+	-	+	+
Drawida willsi	+	+	-	+	+
Eutyphoeus sp.	-	-	-	+	+
Lampito mauritii	+	+	-	+	+
Dendrobaena octoedra	-	+	-	-	-
Eisenia foetida	-	-	-	+	-

Source : Dash and Senapati, 1986.

Maintaining proper temperature

Earthworms regulate the temperature of the soil bioreactor complex through several mechanisms. They strike a proper balance between the endergonic and exergonic bioprocesses to offset the energy fluxes to and from the environment.

Maintaining proper moisture

Earthworms conserve the soil moisture to ensure bacterial processing rather than fungal processing.

TABLE—3.5

Enzyme activity in the guts of earthworms (Mean)

L.mauritii	O.surensis				D.calebi				D.bolaui				
	Ant.	Mid.	Post.	Av.	Ant.	Mid.	Post.	Av.	Ant.	Mid.	Post.	Av.	
Protein (mg)	1.06	0.68	0.59	0.78	0.58	0.46	0.17	0.40	0.38	0.19	0.14	0.24	0.14
Protease*	23.8	32.28	7.71	21.26	12.16	28.69	57.68	32.86	7.88	8.56	10.67	9.04	32.89
Amylase*	75.49	142.45	135.5	117.81	108.38	202.25	284.19	198.27	30.99	43.93	59.68	44.08	258.54
Invertase*	37.98	32.05	41.47	33.84	123.55	209.09	389.05	240.85	36.38	119.18	29.83	61.79	137.01
Cellulase*	16.66	29.48	37.39	27.84	42.10	78.95	119.83	87.69	12.51	20.98	37.76	23.75	141.36
Urease*	0.96	0.77	0.87	0.87	NA	NA	NA	NA	0.22	0.17	0.29	0.23	0.73

* fg/mg protein/h. NA, no activity; Ant., anterior region; Mid., middle region; Post., posterior region; Av., average.

Maintaining proper pH

Earthworm harness acidity to solubilise the ground rock particles, producing nutrients in the form available to the plants. They also have a fine pH-control mechanisms. The soil, too has a pH buffering capacity, which is considerably enhanced by the earthworms.

Provision of nutrients

Major nutrients required for growing bacteria are C, O, N, H, P, K, Na, Ca, Mg, Cl, Fe, etc. While the waste organics are rich sources of carbon, hydrogen, oxygen, they may lack nitrogen and phosphorous.

Nitrogen and phosphorous are provided in the industry by supplying nitrogen and phosphorous compounds. Nitrogen is often provided through organic sources such as soya-meal. Earthworms however provide nitrogen and phosphorous by harnessing selected bacteria which can get nitrogen from air and phosphorus from the rock particles. Rock also supplies best of other elements required by the bacteria.

Provision of oxygen

All clusters need oxygen for respiration, a process which carries out bio-combustion of organics to release nutrients and bioenergy. Bioenergy is temporarily stored and transported within the body through ATP molecules which cut as energy currency.

Vermiculture harness earthworms as bio-aerators which derive their energy from the waste organics. Earthworms, in fact, harness the useful bacteria to consume the waste organics, thus converting wastes into resources.

Biochemical aspects of earthworms

Earthworms contains upto 72% of protein on a dry weight basis. General constitution of an earthworm includes 60-72% protein, 8-17% carbohydrate, 7-9% fat, 4-8% ash, 2-4% minerals with a good range of essential vitamins such as niacin which is a valuable component of animal feed.

Earthworms has a calorific value equal to that of mammalian muscle, with a similar amino acid composition. Its protein is high in the essential aminoacids including those containing sulphur and is of high biological quality. In nature, earthworm forms an important source of protein for a variety of organisms.

Alanine, arginine, aspartic acid, glycine, hydroxy-proline, leucine, tryptophan, histidine, isoleucine and ornithine are predominantly present in the primary amino acid form in all the stages of earthworms, while methionine, proline, tyrosin and valine occur in bound form. Sulphur containing aminoacids are also found in smaller quantities which perform a vital role in growth and metabolism.

Earthworm populations contribute nitrogen to soil through three ways, namely, worm casts, decompostion of dead worms and release of mucus. The organic nitrogen of ingested soil organic matter will be incorporated in the worm biomass during their consummatory behaviour in soil layers. Apart from this, getting mineralised by the symbiotic microbes in the gut and defecated as castings, a part will be used for presynthesis of mucus and released with the soil where it gets decomposed into nitrogen by soil microbes. Dead worms are also subjected to microbial decompostion liberating as inorganic compounds. Thus the organic nitrogen of the ingested organic matter will be cycled and returned to the soil.

Carbohydrate, being the energy reserve seems to be accumulated in juveniles and clitellates, the active stages of growth and reproduction than in the immature non-clitellage worms. Glycogen content ranges from 4 mg/gm weight in the posterior segements to 10 mg in middle segments, with the anterior segments having an intermediate concentration of 6-7 mg/gm. Muscles of the worm also contain measurable amount of glycogen ranging from 3-6 mg/gm in the anterior segments.

Lipid content varies according to seasons and is progressively used up during the developmental process and it also seem to be required for attaining sexual maturity.

Adult earthworms dehydrate at a faster rate than the immature individuals, probably due to their greater activity and discharge of coelomic fluid from the dorsal pores during dessication.

Ash content of an organism is an indication of inorganic elements. Juveniles have high ash content due to their high growth rate. Deviation of ash content in the non-clitellates is more due to a highly varying organic content in this group.

During growth, earthworms maintain the concentration of water, nitrogen, phosphorous and potassium at a steady state level. Copper, cadmium, chromium and nickel accumulate for a short period in the earthworm tissue.

Acid phosphatase activity of cocoon and adult is higher than that of alkaline phosphatase, whereas in young ones alkaline phosphatase have high activity due to the differentiation and histogensis of organs and organ systems.

4

VERMICULTURE

Vermiculture is the production of a stock of earthworms (Hartenstein 1981). It can be described as the scientific method of breeding and rearing earthworms in controlled conditions, it aims at creating favourable conditions, artificially, for the multiplication and the growth of earthworms (Bhole, 1992). It is an innovative type of biotechnology that does not call for expensive laboratories or sophisticated industrial equipment (Bhawalkar 1993).

Vermicomposting is the process by which epigeic earthworm species are used for the conversion of organic wastes into vermicompost, an excellent organic manure or it is the degradation of organic waste by earthwormic consumption (Ashok Kumar 1994). Regular inputs of feed materials for the earthworm can be in the form of agrowastes and kitchen wastes, nitrogen rich materials like cattle dung. By processing wastes into organic fertilizers, organic solid wastes can be treated. Vermicomposting therefore is a solid waste management strategy in which organic solid wastes are considered as resources. (Ismail 1996).

Almost any agricultural, urban or industrial organic material can be used for vermicomposting, but many may need some form of preprocessing to make them acceptable to earthworms. Such preliminary treatments can involve washing, precomposting, macerating or mixing. Ideally, mixtures of several different materials can be processed more readily than individual one, are usually easier to maintain aerobically, and result in a better product. This is primarily due to the wet and sloppy characteristics of some materials, which require the addition of a bulking agent for better handling. According to Seenappa et al (1995) the adaptability of earthworms to different types of organic wastes could be achieved and to make such wastes more palatable the waste has to be aerated in rotor drums in order to encourage aerobic microbes before feeding the waste to earthworms. Thus the common solution is *pretreatment* or *processing* or *precomposting* (Bhiday 1995, Edwards 1995, Abbasi and Ramasamy 1997)

CRITERIA FOR THE SELECTION OF SPECIES SUITABLE FOR VERMICOMPOSTING

The species of earthworms used for the process of vermicomposting must possess a few basic characteristics, in order to attain the objectives of vermicomposting:

(i) occurrence in high percentage;

(ii) wide adaptability for environmental variations;

(iii) high metabolic demand, presence of digestive enzymes like cellulase, chitinase, high assimilation and production efficiency;

(iv) high fecundity, low incubation period, short development period with high growth rate.

The above selection of the earthworm species is possible by field and laboratory information based on :

(i) distribution dynamics and niche separation;

(ii) feeding and reproductive strategy;

(iii) metabolic demand;

(iv) secondary production and bioenergetic strategy.

Four endemic species have been certified for Vermicomposting, They are *Dichogaster bolaui, Drawida willsi, Lampito mauritii* and *Perionyx excavatus* (Senapati 1993).

SPECIES USED IN VERMICOMPOSTING

A number of species of earthworms have been used in

Vermicomposting. The one most commonly used worldwide is *Eisenia foetida*, the tiger or brandling worm. Other suitable species include *Lumbricus rubellus*, the red worm; *Eudrilus eugeniae*, the African night crawler and *Perionyx excavatus*, an Asian species. The latter two species do well but cannot withstand low temperatures. It is generally known that the epigeic species *Eudrilus eugeniae, Perionyx excavatus*, and *Eisenia foetida* have a potential as waste decomposers. (Hartenstein et al 1979. Graff 1974). The best choice for vermicomposting are two epigeic species, *Eudrilus eugeniae* and *Eisenia foetida*. (Ashok Kumar 1994). These are found to assimilate 5-10% of the ingested material and the rest is excreted out as loose granular cast coated with mucopolysaccharides which act as the important sub strate for aerobic microbes to utilize for their metabolic activities (Seenappa and Kale 1995)

THE BASIS OF VERMICOMPOSTING

The principles behind vermicomposting are relatively simple and related to those involved in traditional composting. Certain species of earthworms can consume organic residuals very rapidly and fragment them into much finer particles by passing them through a grinding gizzard, an organ that all earthworm possess. The earthworms derive their nourishment from the microorganisms that grow upon the organic materials. At the same time, they promote further microbial activity in the residuals so that the faecal material or 'casts' that they produce, is much more fragmented and microbially active than what the earthworms consume. During this process, the important plant nutrients in the organic material—particularly nitrogen, phosphorus, potassium and calcium—are released and converted through microbial action into forms that are much more soluble and available to plants than those in the parent compounds (Edwards 1995).

The retention time of the waste in the earthworm is short. Worms can digest several times their own weight each day, and large quantities are passed through an average population of earthworms. In the traditional aerobic composting process, the organic materials have to be turned regularly or aerated in some way in order to maintain aerobic conditions. This often may involve extensive engineering to process the residuals as rapidly as possible on a large scale. In vermicomposting, the earthworms—which survive only under aerobic conditions—take over both the roles of turning and maintaining the organics in an aerobic condition, thereby lessening the need for expensive engineering.

The major constraint to vermicomposting is that, in contrast to traditional composting (a thermophilic process that can raise temperature in the waste to more than 70°C), vermicomposting systems must be maintained at temperatures below 35°C. Exposure of the earthworms to temperatures above this, even for short periods, will kill them. Avoidance of such overheating, requires careful management. Earthworms are active and consume organic materials in a relatively narrow layer of 6-9 inches below the surface of a compost heap or bed. The key to successful vermicomposting lies in adding materials to the surface of piles or beds in thin, successive layers so that heating does not become excessive. The heating, however, should be sufficient to maintain the activity of the earthworms at a high level of efficiency. The processing of organic materials occurs most rapidly at temperatures between 15°C and 25°C (60° F to 79°F). and at moisture contents of 70% to 90%. Outside these limits, earthworm activity and productivity, and thus the rate of waste processing, falls off dramatically. For maximum efficiency, the feedstock should be maintained as close to these environmental limits as possible. (Edwards 1995).

STEPS INVOLVED IN VERMICOMPOSTING

Composting can be done either in pits or concrete tanks or well rings or in wooden or plastic crates appropriate to a given situation. It is preferable to select a composting site under shade, in the upland or an elevated level, to prevent water stagnation in pits during rains.

Vermicomposting is set up by first placing a basal layer of vermibed comprising of broken bricks or pebbles (3-4 cms) followed by a layer of coarse sand to a total thickness of 6-7 cms to ensure proper drainage. This is followed by a 15 cms moist layer of loamy soil as sshown in Figure 4.1 Into this soil are inoculated about 100 locally collected earthworms (about 50 surface and 50 subsurface varieties). Small lumps of cattledung (fresh or dry) are then scattered over the soil and covered with a 10 cm layer of hay. Water is sprayed till the entire set up is moist but not wet. Less water kills the worms and too much chases them away. The unit is kept covered with broad leaves like those of coconut or palmyrah. Old jute bags can also be used for covering. Watering the unit is continued and the unit is monitored for 30 days. The appearance of juvenile earthworms by this time is a healthy sign. Organic refuse is added from the thirty-first day as a spread on the bed after removing the fronds The spread should not exceed 5 cms in thickness at each application. Though addition of this amount of matter can be done everyday, it is advisable for a beginner to spread only twice a week, watering to requirement. After a few applications, the refuse is turned ones without disturbing the bed. The day, enough refuse has been added into the unit, watering is done and 45 days later the compost is ready for harvest.

As the organic refuse changes into a dark brown compost addition of water is stopped (42nd day). This moves the worms into the vermibed. The compost is harvested and the harvested compost is placed in the form of a cone on ground in bright sunlight. This will facilitate worms present in the compost to move to the lower layers. The compost pile is spread for about 24 to 36 hours, the worms are removed from the lower layers of the compost (Ismail 1996). Vermicomposting mainly involves three phases:

1) collection of wastes, mechanical separation of metal, glass, ceramics etc. and storage. Shredding helps in increasing surface area by fragmentaion, and thus makes it more homogenous;

2) Earthworm inoculation;

3) Screening and sorting of larger non-decomposed waste which could be used for reprocessing or land filling.

Vermitechnology for waste land conservation by employing anecic and endogeic earthworms is relatively a new concept. The concept is based on the fact that anecic and endogeic worms are conservative in comparison to epigeics.

For example epigeic worm *Dichogaster bolaui* measuring about 4 cm adult size, 6-8 mg dry body weight with phytophagous habit, surface living at 0-3 cm, could utilize about 2.4 KJ/g dry wt/ day whereas *Polypheretima elongata*, an endogeic species with about 9-30 cm adult size, 300-400 mg dry weight, with geophagous habit, deep soil living (below 30-40 cm soil depth) could utilize only 0.6 KJ/ g dry wt/day. Period of activity is only about 142 days for *D. bolaui*

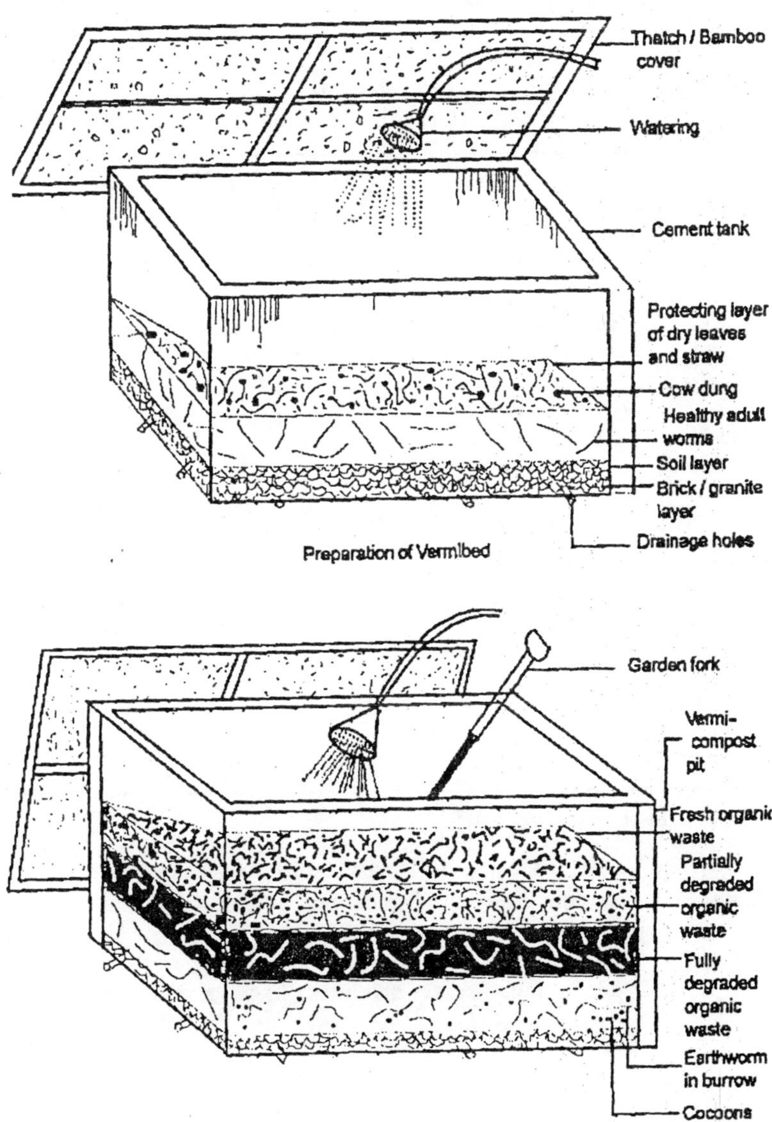

Fig. 4.1: Stages of Vermicomposting Process

whereas it is 365 days for *P. elongata* per year. Annually *D. boulaui* and *P. elongata* contributed about 237 and 723 KJ/n^2 towards nitrogenous excretory products including urea, ammonia, uric acid, amino acids and proteins (mucus), of which mucus only comprised more than 50%.

TABLE—4.1

Vermicultural characteristics of some Indian earthworms

Soil temp. for maxi- mum growth	*Age for cocoon produc- tion in weeks*	*Upper limit of soil temp. tolerance*	*Vermi- stabiliz- ation time in weeks °C*	*No. of young/ cocoon*	*Incuba- tion period in weeks*	*Average size in g.*	
Eisenia foetida	18 - 25	5 - 9	125	6 - 8	2 - 4	3 - 4	0.5
Eudrillus eugeinae	20 - 25	7 - 10	30	3 - 4	2 - 3	4	1
Perionyx excavatus	25 - 30	15 - 18	30	4 - 5	1	4	1
Lampito mauritii	18 - 30	8 - 10	30	3.0	1	4	1
Octochaetona surensis	20 - 25	15 - 20	27	8 - 10	1	4	1
Drawida willsi	20 - 25	6 - 10	30	3 - 4	2 - 3	2	0.5

Source : Dash and Senapati (1985).

The Vermicultural characteristics of earthworms from different parts of the world are given in the Table 4.1 Table 4.2 Vermitechnology is the application of earthworms in:

i) producing useful products like vermifertiliser, worm tissue for animal feed etc;

ii) monitoring of the environment for soil fertility, organic matter, heavy metal, non-biodegradable toxic material pollution etc; and

iii) maintenance of environmental quality.

TABLE—4.2

Vermicultural characteristics of earthworms from different parts of the world

Worm species	Soil temperature for maximum growth in °C	Age for cocoon production in weeks	Upper limit of soil temperature tolerance in °C	Vermi Stabilisation in weeks	No. of young(s) cocoon	Incubation period in week(s)	Size in g (live wt)
L. rubellus	15 - 18	8 - 9	-	-	1	16	2.00
L. terrestris	15 - 18	14 - 15	-	-	1	25 -30	10.00
D. veneta	20 - 25	5 - 6	-	-	1	-	4.00
P. hawayana	25	5 - 6	-	-	1	-	2.60
E. foetida	18 - 25	5 - 9	25	6 - 8	2 - 4	3 - 4	0.50
E. eugeniae	20 - 25	7 - 10	30	3 - 4	2 - 3	4	1.00
P. excavatus	25 - 30	15 - 18	30	4 - 5	1	4	1.00
D. bolaui	25 - 30	5 - 9	31	3	1 - 2	1	0.04
O. occidentalis	23 - 27	-	30	3 - 4	-	-	0.03
D. willisi	2 - 25	6 - 10	33	3 - 4	2 - 3	2	0.15
O. surensis	20 - 25	15 - 20	27	8 -10	1	4	1.00
L. mauritii	18 - 30	8 - 10	30	3	1	4	1.00
M. elongata	23 - 27	20 - 24	28	8 -10	1	4	3.50

Vermitechnology can be considered in two aspects. One is vermicomposting which helps in enhancing organic manure production through earthwormic consumption and thus is helpful in managing waste biomass. The second aspect is for reclamation or convertion of waste by managing anecic and endogeic category of earthworms. (Senapati 1993). The earthworms suitable for vermicomposting have different characteristics than those suitable for application in vermiconservation, as shown in Table 4.3

CULTURING TECHNIQUES

Generally, the breeding boxes, the feed material, bedding material etc, vary from breeder to breeder. The essential factors like optimum temperature, optimum moisture, readily ingestible feed material, drainage, aeration, protection from predators are to be considered, again these being subjective , relative to the earthworm species, the location and available resources. Here are a few examples:

1. According to Dash and Senapati(1986 a,b), earthworms can be cultured in wooden boxes of 50 x 25 x 25 cms size. One fourth of the box is filled with soil with a layer of gravel at the base. One fourth of the box is filled with sawdust or ricebran or straw or sieved organic garbage. One fourth with dry cow dung or any other nitrogenous waste. The rest one fourth of the box is to be left empty. Initially, one hundred adult earthworms can grow to 150 to 200 times in a six month culture. The soil moisture to be maintained at about 15-20%, temperature of 25 to 28 degree celcius is suitable for tropical species.

2. Deepak Suchde has developed the indoor nursery technique for the breeding of the earthworm species *Eisenia foetida*. In this vermicultural technique, the earthworms are raised in empty wooden boxes or plastic trays measuring 37.5 x 60 x 22.5 cms.

Approximately half a teaspoon of lime is sprinkled over the base and a layer of waste paper is spread on it . A 2.5 cm layer of fully decomposed manure along with groundnut shells is added on the top. About 100 earthworms are introduced into the centre and the whole assembly is placed in a cool place. From the second day onwards, two table spoons of fresh cowdung is added daily at the centre.

TABLE—4.3

Comparative characteristic features of a vermicomposting and vermicon versing earthworm

Characteristics	Vermicomposting example:Dichogaster bolaui	Vermiconserving example:Polyphereima elongata
1	2	3
1. Habitat characteristics		
(a) Habitat	Surface living with high organic content (more than 10g %)	Deep dwelling in mineral with low organic content (less than 5g % 19-30)
(b) Soil temperature (°C)	18 - 32	19 - 30
(c) Soil moisture (g%)	01 - 25	06 - 29
(d) Habit	Phytophaguas (plant feeding)	Geophagus (soil eating)
(e) Stratification (cm) (60% of total population)	0 - 5	15 - 40
2. Biological characteristics		
(a) Length (mm)	19 - 43	95 - 300
(b) Diameter (mm)	1 - 3	3 - 6
(c) Total segments	70 - 98	136 - 297
(d) Coloration	Palebrown,dark in dorsal side	no coloration
(e) Clitellum (segment)	Saddle shaped (v-vii)	Ring shaped (XIV-XVI)
(f) Prostomium	Procpilobous	lipilobous

{Cont.}...

	1	2	3
(g)	Gizzard (segment)	Two nos (4/5 and 7/8)	Absent
(h)	Typhlosole	Absent or redimentary	Present, Lamelliform
(i)	Calciferous gland	Present	Absent
(j)	Live weight (g/adult)	0.03-0.04	3.0 - 4.5
(k)	Dry weight (g/adult)	0.006-0.008	0.3 - 0.45
(l)	Moisture content	80	90
(m)	Burrowing muslces	Reduced	Developed
(n)	Regeneration	Most frequent	Nil
(o)	Period of activity	4-5 months. (Jan. IV week to Oct. IV week)	Throught the year
(p)	Sensitivity of pH (acidic range)	Lower (tolerance 4.5-6.5)	Higher (tolerance 6.5-7.5)
(q)	Sensitivity to light	Lower	Higher
(r)	Avoidance of deciccation	By quiescence (diapause)	By quiescence(no diapause)
(s)	Mobility	Rapid	Feeble
(t)	Incubation period of cocoon.	7 - 10 days	28 - 31 days
(u)	Period of maturity (hatching to adult)	About one month	About 5 months
(v)	Duration of reproducitive life	Short (15 - 30 days)	Long (200-400 days)
(w)	Number of young hatched per cocoon	Higher (more than one)	Lower (usually one)

{Cont.}...

1	2	3
(x) Time distribution of mortality	Shorter	Longer
(y) Form of survisorship	Type-III	Type-I & II
(z) Seasonal stability of population	Least (unimodal)	High (multimodal)
(a') Feeding rate (intestinal rate)	Slow	Rapid
(b') Rate of respiration	High	Low
Total respiration (R) (Kl, $m^{-2}yr^{-1}$)	405.52	899.06
Respiration rate (Kl g dry tissue^{-1}yr^{-1})	141.67	75.12
(c') Rate of excretion	High	Low
Total excretion(E) (Kl, $m^{-2}yr^{-1}$).	286.76	722.65
Excretion rate (Kl,g dry tissue^{-2}yr^{-1})	99.67	75.12
(d') Average earthworm biomass(B) dry wt. fortnight^{-1}(Kl,m^{-2}, fortnight^{-1})	2.87(55.50)	9.2 (186.04)
(e') Tissue production rate	High	Low
Total tissue production (Kl, m^{-2}, yr^{-1})	224.4	407.24

(Cont.)...

1		2	3
	Production rate (KI,g dry tissue $^{-1}$yr^{-1})	78.2	42.33
(f')	Tissue utilised in cocoon production	High	Low
	Total cocoon produced (KI,m^{-2}, yr^{-1})	53.05	24.83
	(KI, g dry tissue^{-1} yr^{-1})	18.50	2.58
(g')	Rate of secondary production (p)	High	Low
	Total secondary production (KI,m^{-2}yr^{-1})	227.44	432.07
	Rate of secondary production (KI,g dry tissue^{-1}yr^{-1})	79.25	44.91
(h')	Percentage contribution to secondary production by		
	(i) Tissue production	80.9	94.3
	(ii) Tissue utilized in reproduction	19.1	5.7
(i')	Total energy utilisation (kj g dry tissue^{-1}, dry^{-1}	2.5	
(j')	Biomass turn over p,B^{-1}	5.0	

{Cont.}...

	1	2	3
(k')	Worm cast production(times live body Wt.day $^{-1}$)	Low (1-2)	High (5-10)
	Cast stability	Low	High
	Dispersion in water	Quick	Late
	Mucus content of cast	Less	High
(l')	Oxygen affinity of haemo--globin	Low	High
	Resistance to anexia or hypoxia	Low	High
(m')	Decomposition enzyme (cellulase)	Present	Absent
(n')	Mechanism of interaction with matter	Biodegradation (mineralisation)	Bio-conversion of nutrients (Immobilisation) and Macro-structure development
(o')	Application in vermi-culture technology	Vermi-composting	Vermi-conservation

Source : Senapati B.K., 1993.

After two weeks of regular feeding, the worms are seen to produce conoons and young ones emerge after three weeks. Over this a waste paper is placed and 2.5cms of bedding material along with the daily quota of fresh cowdung, half a tablespoon of ground pulse residues is added, twice a week. The trays can be covered with 0.5 cm thickness of partially decomposed rice straw. After three months the population of earthworms should be enough to transfer them to 10 such boxes.

3. On a more commercial level, Bio-genik systems in Bombay, sell 'ready made' vermiculture breeder boxes of *Eisenia foetida*. The container is a five-ply corrugated box (size 9 .5 x 9.5 x 4.75 inches) lined with a plastic sheet. A soilless medium, to hold the earthworms in various stages viz. cocoons to adults, is especially prepared, moistened. The medium is mixed with the 'special earthworm food' to last for four weeks. Intermittent moistening is required.

4. Dr. Radha Kale of UAS, Bangalore, successfully breeds *Eudrilus eugeniae*. The containers to house the earthworms can be shallow cement tanks, wooden boxes, stone line pits or plastic tubs of 1 x 1 x 0.3mts. This size container can accomodate 2000 worms.

The worms have to be cultured in warm moist places, with precautions against direct sunlight, heavy rainfall, predators such as ants, birds, rats. The base material can be a few mm layer of saw dust or coconut husk. The feeding material can be the dung of cattle, horses, pigs or poultry droppings mixed with kitchen wastes, leaf litter. The feeding material is made to undergo decomposition for 7-10 days, prior to the introduction of the earthworms. The earth worms excrete the unassimilated material as loose granular vermicastings at the surface, usually away from the food source. The vermicastings have to be brushed aside and collected. The collected vermicastings are then gathered into conical heaps and left overnight, during this period the earthworms move down to the lower layers of the heaps. The upper layers of the coned vermicastings which are free of the worms, are removed, air-dried lightly and sieved using a 3 mm sieve to separate the cocoons and the juveniles. The dried,sieved castings are ready for use.

5. Dr Narayan, from Aurobrindavan, Pondicherry, rears earthworm species of *Eudrilus eugeniae.* Dr Narayan suggests, a 3 cms high layer of sawdust, followed by a 3 cms high layer of river sand, follwed by a 3 cms high layer of loamy soil, to form the vermibed for the earthworms. The earthworms are introduced into the moistened vermibed. The earthworms are fed with cowdung.

Dr. Narayan uses cowdung as feed material for the earthworms, because according to him, cowdung is easily and readily available. The cowdung is placed in centre of the vermibed, so as to induce the earthworms to cast near the .outer edges, thus helping in the removal of the vermicastings periodically. The collected vermicastings are heaped, and shade dried for the few hours, then sieved through a 2 mm sieve. Sieving ensures that the cocoons, juveniles are screened and retained.

6. This author and coworkers Bhavna Mahadeviah and E.V.Ramasamy found that a layer of saw dust with 3 cm deep layer of river sand over it and another 3 cm deep layer of garden soil form a cosy vermibed. The bed must be kept well-moist or the earthworms either run away or die from dehydration.

The food material for the worms (cowdung, leaf litter, weeds etc) should be evenly spread over the vermibed taking care that anoxic conditions do not develop.

FACTORS INFLUENCING THE CULTURING OF EARTHWORMS

Several factors control the culturing and maintenance of healthy earthworm populations, of which the most important are :

1. Food
2. Hydrogen ion concentration
3. Moisture
4. Temperature
5. Light
6. Protection from predators

Food

One of the most important factors that control the establishment and continuity of earthworm populations is food and its quantity. Higher nitrogen ratios help in faster growth and greater production of cocoons. Fresh green matter is not easily fed upon. Decomposition by microbial activity is essential before earthworms can feed on fresh waste.

The Carbon-Nitrogen (C:N) ratio is the critical factor that limits earthworm populations. When the C:N ratio of the feed material increases, it becomes difficult to extract enough nitrogen for tissue production. Earthworms find it difficult to survive when the organic carbon content of the soil is low.

Moisture

Moisture levels have to be maintained at around 50% so that the microbial activity is high and the food matter is easy to feed upon. Excess water leads to anaerobic conditions which in turn lowers the pH and creates acidic conditions.

Acidic conditions reduce productivity and cause migration.

Temperature

The temperature should be maintained around 20-30°c. Temperature affects metabolism, growth and reproduction. Soils exposed to the sun lose moisture quickly and are usually devoid of earthworms. Earthworms maintain lower body temperatures than the surrounding soil or organic matter by their metabolic adjustments.

Light

Earthworms are very sensitive to light. The photo receptor cells detect light and the earthworm moves away to avoid strong light. The deep burrowing anecics and other species emerge at the surface only at night for this reason.

Hydrogen ion concentration (pH)

Earthworms are sensitive to changes in pH. They prefer conditions of neutral reaction. Earthworms find it difficult to survive if the pH falls below 6 and either migrate or are killed.

Predators

Earthworms are preyed upon by many species of ants, birds, toads, salamanders, snakes, moles, cats, rats, dogs etc. Moles catch earthworms, bite off three to five anterior segments to prevent locomotion and keep them in their burrows. A variety of invertebrates also feed on earthworms. These include flatworms, centipedes, staphylinid beetles, etc.

BENEFITS AND DRAWBACKS OF VERMICOMPOSTING

Vermicomposting can break down organic residuals into valuable, finely divided plant growth media with excellent porosity, aeration and water holding capacity, rich in available nutrients with superior plant growth characteristics.

The major drawback of vermicomposts is that the organics do not go through a high temperature phase, so if materials containing pathogens are used, they may need an additional precomposting phase or sterilization process, to ensure that the pathogens are killed. There is, however, considerable scientific evidence that human pathogens do not survive the vermicomposting process.

5

PRESENT STATUS OF SOLID WASTE GENERATION AND DISPOSAL

K. Senthilvelan*

TYPES AND QUANTITIES OF SOLID WASTE GENERATED

From Chapter 1, one can get an idea about the quantity of the waste that is being generated. The per capita municipal waste generation in some cities is shown in Table 5.1. In developing countries, the wastes are mostly organic, and are biodegradable in nature. Table 5.2 shows the potential waste biomass in India and Figure 5.1 gives the characteristics of a typical Indian city refuse. The wastes of the developed countries have large proportions of non-biodegradable organics like plastic and inorganics including metals (Figure 5.2.)

OVERVIEW OF SOLID WASTE TREATMENT AND DISPOSAL TECHNIQUES

Some of the common methods used for the treatment and disposal of solid wastes are :

(i) Open dumping

(ii) Landfilling

* Er. K. Senthilvelan, M.E, Ph.D is a Scientist with Centre for Pollution Control and Energy Technology.

(iii) Incineration

(iv) Anaerobic digestion

(v) Composting

Open dumping

Low lying areas are generally chosen, into which the waste are deposited , left uncovered, creating nuisance of odour, vectors, endangering public health, possible contamination of groundwater and soil.

TABLE—5.1
Per captia municipal waste generation in some selected cities

City	*Kg/head/ day*	*City*	*K g/head/ day*
Mumbai	0.5	Bangkok, Thailand	0.45
Calcutta	0.5	Manila,Phillipines	0.5
Average of Indian Cities	0.15 to 0.35	Hong Kong	0.85
Kathmandu, Nepal	0.25	Singapore	0.87
Rangoon, Burma	0.25	Washington, USA	1.97 (1958) 2.16 (1968)
Colombo, Sri Lanka	0.42	Los Angeles, USA	2.09 (1958) 3.15 (1968)

Source : CEE, Bangalore.

Land filling

Landfill is the term used to describe a properly designed and controlled operation for land disposal of waste (Wilson 1981, Hinricks 1992). The waste is spread and compacted into layers not exceeding 2.5m in depth and is then covered with soil to depth not less than 15cm.When the landfill site is full, a final layer of soil tó a minimum depth of 1m is needed. Since the waste is covered its limits the vectors,the spreading of the waste by the wind, odour problems and does not create an eye sore.

In the beginning, the decomposition process is predominantly aerobic; the end products are carbon-dioxide and water. But once the entrapped oxygen is consumed, the decomposition process turns anaerobic, the end products of which are methane and carbon-dioxide. Here lies one of the potential hazards of landfills—if the gas escapes, there may be odour problems associated with the sulphur components. If the gas is restricted, a potential fire or explosion hazard may be created. Another problem associated with landfills is the infiltration of water by precipitation, water already present in the waste, water generated by biodegradation can carry the leachate of the landfill laterally or vertically and the leachate can find its way into groundwater and/or surface water bringing about contamination.With landfilling one more restriction is the availability of land area. For example, Mumbai has four landfill sites, which are estimated to get filled up within 10 to 15 years,therefore, after the present sites get filled, other alternatives have to be looked into.

Incineration

Incineration technology was introduced as early as 1885. Primarily incinerators were used to reduce the volume of waste prior to disposal. Incineration involves the combustion of the wastes under controlled conditions of temperature, air, gas turbulence, residence time etc. The volume of the waste is said to be greatly reduced, some put it at 80 - 90%, but it must be noted that it applies to the waste that can be incinerated.

A problem with incineration is that the residual ash and that which escapes with the flue are toxic containing most of the toxic metals. In addition a number of toxic compounds are actually created with the fly ash particles acting as nuclei in a process called post - combustion formation, eg. dioxins and furans which are highly toxic. (Connett and Connett 1994.)

Anaerobic Digestion

Anaerobic digestion is basically decomposition of the waste in anaerobic conditions (low in oxygen) by anaerobic microorganisms. The end products are methane gas which is used as a fuel, and the digested sludge is commonly applied to agricultural fields. Supposing the starting material is mainly cellulosic in nature, then the first step in anaerobic digestion is hydrolysis, the second step is the conversion of carbohydrates, proteins and fats into short-chain fatty acids by

TABLE—5.2

Potential of Waste Biomass in India

Organic	Quantity in lakh tonnes per annum	Plant nutrients in thousand tonnes			Total
		N	P_2O_2	K_2O	
1. Animal waste/ by products	17043.2	4111.9	1298.6	1952.0	7362.5
2. Crop residues/ by products	1599.5	810.9	562.7	2085.4	3459.0
3. Fruit and Vegetable wastes/residues	0.3	0.2	0.1	0.2	0.5
4. Forest residues/by products	175.0	243.6	34.4	98.8	376.8
5. Fish and marine wastes/residues	0.5	3.4	2.9	0.5	6.8
6. Human habitation wastes	3194.8	815.5	322.1	248.8	1386.4
7. Aquatic biomass/other wastes	30.0	60.0	30.0	60.0	150.0
8. Biofertilizers (Rhizobium, non legumes, Blue gree algae)	640.0	1225.0	—	—	1225.0

Source: Vimal and Talshilkar, 1982.

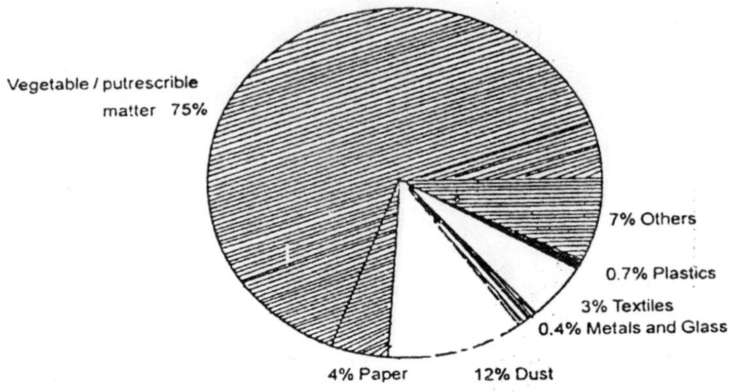

Fig. 5.1. Characteristics of an Indian City refuse (Source CEE, Bangalore)

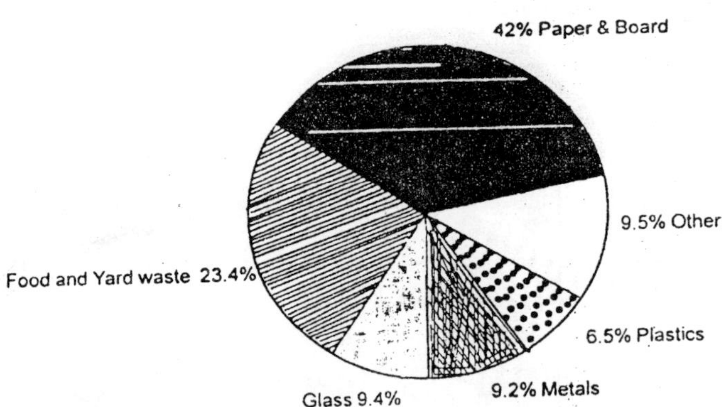

Fig. 5.2 Characteristics of municipal solid waste in USA
(Source Hinricks, 1992)

acidogenic bacteria. The short chain fatty acids are inturn converted into acetates and bicarbonates by acetogens, this is the third step. The fourth step is the conversion of acetates and bicarbonates into carbondioxide and methane. The parameters that need to be considered during anaerobic digestion are :

(i) Temperature, which may be held in the mesophilic range (40°C) or thermophilic range (60°C);

(ii) The maintenance of anaerobic conditions;

(iii) pH range of 6.7 - 7.0;

(iv) Nutrients supplied to the microorganisms for optimum growth.

(v) Toxicity of the input wastes should be minimised.

Composting

The process of sanitary disposal and the reclamation of organic material is termed as composting. This process uses microorganisms to degrade the waste organic matter. The main steps are :

Preparation

Preparation of the waste for subjecting it to composting involves the separation of the organic and inorganic parts of the waste. Also nutrients like Nitrogen may be required, if found deficient in the parent material, to feed the microorganisms, and to hasten decomposition.

Digestion

Digestion involves most of the micro-biological action. The prepared waste is piled in windrows. The wastes are regularly turned to ensure adequate aeration, by preferably a purpose-built turning machine. Digestion can take about three weeks.

Curing

Curing allows for the decomposition of the remaining cellulose and lignin, which has not been digested. About three months is the curing period.

Finishing

Finishing is basically screening, to remove remaining inorganics, drying, grinding and pelletization of compost, ready for marketing.

The compost is sold as organic manure to farmers, horticulturists etc, But necessary precautionary measures have to be adopted in order to avoid the problems associated with the compost; often the compost is not cured sufficiently and the parent waste material may not have been segregated properly, so the compost can be contaminated by various toxic materials such as PCBs (Polychlorinated Biphenyls), solvents, pesticides, heavy metals from batteries (mercury, cadmium, zinc), leather (chromium), paper (lead), cosmetics (cadmium and zinc) and also physical contaminants such as plastic and glass.

ILLUSTRATIVE EXAMPLES OF PRESENT SOLID WASTE DISPOSAL STRATEGIES IN INDIA

The managament of waste involves collection, transfer, processing, treatment and disposal. Each of the element has been described in the Table 5.3. In the Indian scenario, as can be seen from Table 5.4 which shows the levels of service in some Indian cities, only about 60% of the generated wastes are collected for possible treatment and disposal.

Faced with increasing quantity of garbage and with the landfill sites rapidly filled,the Municipal Corporations are trying alternative treatment and disposal methods to the traditional open dumping and landfilling methods. Taking the Bombay Municipal Corporation (BMC), as an example, presently, part of the garbage is being processed into fuel pellets.Part of the garbage is being planned to be processed into vermicompost and it is hoped that 200 tons of garbage can be 'vermi-processed' everyday. The process is said to take about six weeks for the conversion and the product is being test marketed as a bio-organic soil enricher.

Community bin system

The community bin system is usually practised in India wherein individuals deposit their waste in bins located at street corners and at specific intervals. Various types of vehicles, varying from bullock carts to compactors are used for transportation. However, the general-purpose open body trucks of 5 to 7 tonnes capacity are in common use. In the smaller towns, tractor-trailers are used despite being noisy and inefficient. In a few cities, compactor vehicles are also being used. These vehicles are able to provide a compaction ration of only 1.25 to 1.5, have high capital cost and require extensive maintenance. The recent trend is towards use of container-carriers and dumper placers wherein the containers of the vehicles are themselves used as community bins. A vehicle with an empty container, on reaching the collection point, unloads the empty container and then lifts the container filled with solid waste and carries it to the disposal site. In such a system, the vehicles make 5 to 6 trips per day as compared to 1-2 trips per day made by the other vehicles as the former use the truck as a prime mover, instead of tractor. The transport volume is usually expressed in terms of cubic meter per million population. Available transport volume as obtained in 44 Indian cities is indicated in the Table 5.5. Over 80% of the cities are provided with 100 to 400m^3 of transport volume provided. If the waste is to be removed to the disposal site every day, the minimum transport volume required is 850m^3 million population. If available transport vehicles make 2 trips/day, the minimum transport volume requirement is 425m^3/million population. Thus the existing volume is inadequate resulting in removal of only a part of the generated waste.

TABLE—5.3

Description of the functional elements of a solid waste management system

Functional element	*Description*
Waste generation	Those activities in which materials are identified as no longer living of value and are either thrown away or gathered together for disposal
On-site handling, storage and processing	Those activities associated with the handling, storage and processing of solid waste at or near the point of generation.
Collection	Those activities associated with the gathering of solid waste and the hauling of waste after collection vehicle is emptied.
Transfer and transport	Those activities associated with (1) the transfer of waste from the smaller collection vehicle to the larger transport equipment and (2) the subsequent transport of the wastes, usually over long distance, to the disposal site.
Processing and recovery	Those techniques, equipment and facilities used both to improve the efficiency of the other functional elements and to recover usable materials, conversion products, or energy from solid waste.

Disposal	Those activities associated with ultimate disposal of solid waste, including those wastes collected and transported directly to a landfill site, semisolid wastes (sludge) from wastewater treatment plants, incinerator residue, compost, or other substances from the various solid-waste processing plants that are of no further use.

(Peavy et al 1985)

Usually 4-6 workers are deployed with every transport vehicle. A majority of solid waste transport vehicles are more than 7 years old. The average trip distance is less than 20 km. The waste is transported mostly by municipal vehicles, though in some large towns, private vehicles are also hired to augment the fleet size. The maintenance of the vehicles is carried out in the general municipal workshop along with other municipal vehicles where the municipal refuse vehicles receive the last priority. Most of these workshops have facilities for minor repairs only.

TABLE—5.4

Solid waste management. Levels of service in some towns—Solid waste per day

Town	Population (1981)	Solid Waste		Collection efficiency
		Generated (Tons)	Collected (Tons)	(%)
Bombay	8,227,332	3200	3100	96.9
Madras	4,276,635	1819	1637	90.0
Bangalore	2,913,537	1800	1225	68.1
Ahmedabad	2,515,195	1200	1080	90.0
Kanpur	1,688,424	2142	1500	70.0
Pune	1,685,300	1000	700	70.0
Lucknow	1,006,530	600	500	83.3
	Total	11761	9742	82.8
Coimbatore	917,155	175	113	64.6
Madurai	904,362	310	160	51.6
Indore	827,071	120	100	83.3
Baroda	744,043	312	193	60.0
Cochin	685,686	230	120	52.2
Bhopal	672,329	321	300	93.5
Tiruchi	607,815	130	60	46.2
Calicut	546,060	200	75	37.5

Meerut	538,461	120	70	58.3
Hubli-Dharwad	526,493	75	60	80.0
Trivandrum	519,766	120	75	62.5
Salem	515,021	130	25	19.2
Mysore	476,446	204	122	60.0
Thane	388,577	350	200	57.1
Jamnagar	317,037	149	89	60.0
Gulbarga	218,621	10	8	80.0
Sambalpur	162,190	60	36	60.0
	Total	3016	1806	59.0
Anand	83,815	34	17	50.0
Kalore	69,794	16	8	50.0
Bhuj	69,730	27	14	50.0
Baripada	52,992	30	28	93.3
Panvel	37,026	6	4	66.7
Khopoli	32,108	6	3	50.0
Koraput	31,644	11	6	50.0
Dehgam	24,817	9	4	44.4
Mehmedabad	22,297	9	4	44.4

Source: CEE, Bangalore.

TABLE—5.5

Transport volume* available in different Indian cities**

Transport Volume	*% of Cities*
< 100	4.54
100 - 200	34.10
200 - 300	29.55
300 - 400	25.00
> 400	6.81

* m3/million population

** 44 cities surveyed

Source : Neeri Reports

The composting process should function in confined quarters, control odours and leachate, and provide optimal conditions for decomposition, because the faster the decomposition, the lesser the space needed (Outerbridge 1991).

6

COMPOSTING AND VERMICOMPOSTING

Composting is the process of converting organic residues of plant and animal origin into manure rich in humus and plant nutrients. It can also be defined as the bioconversion of organic wastes into an amorphous dark brown to black colloidal humus like substance under conditions of optimum temperature, moisture and aeration.

It is largely a microbiological process based upon the activities of a host of bacteria, actinomycetes, and fungi. All kinds of organic residues amenable to the enzymatic activities of the microorganisms can be converted into compost by providing optimum conditions for biodegradation. Unless strictly controlled, composting employs the activities of both aerobic and anaerobic microorganisms.

Effective harnessing of the great biochemical activities of microorganisms for bioconversion processes have become imperative today as modern societies are generating huge quantities of wastes. Unless these wastes are prudently managed and recycled, not only will the dwindling resources become further scarce, but environmental quality will also deteriorate to an intolerable level. In this background, conversion of organic wastes into value-added products through microbial technologies appears to be an extremely useful approach.

In the entire areas of waste recycling composting emerges as the most widely applicable process for handling diverse waste (HLS Tandon, 1994).

Methods of Composting

Basically, any system or design that ensures efficient decomposition of organic matter can constitute a composting method. Conventionally, two methods of composting are known in India. A brief description of these methods are given below.

Indore Method

This method was worked out by Sir Albert Howard, a British agronomist in India, at Indore in Madhya Pradesh during 1924-30. Basically, it was a systematization of the traditional composting practices being followed in China and India for centuries (Howard 1933). The Indore method is an aerobic process and hence precludes adequate supply of oxygen during the decomposition process. Waste organic materials such as straw, garbage, leaves and plant clippings are laid in a heap or pit in alternate layers with animal manure and soil. Accordingly, a 15cm thick and 1.5-12.0 m wide layer of organic materials to be composted is placed on a hard upland place. This is followed by a 4-5 cm layer of animal-manure (dung), which is in turn covered by a sprinkling of surface soil mixed with a small quantity of lime or wood ashes, about 30mm in all. The layers are repeated until the heap reaches a height of 1.5 - 2.0 m. The final layer should be of the compostable material covered by a thin layer of soil, about 60mm. To provide optimum moisture (60-70%), water is sprinkled over each layer. The same procedure is followed if composting is carried out in pits of about 1 m deep, 1.5-2.0 m wide, and of suitable length. The heap is turned thoroughly at intervals of 3,6 and 12 weeks. The finished compost is ready in about three months if the materials are properly shredded and layered. Generally, it takes about four months for the compost to be ready. The Indore method has the disadvantage that it demands considerable labour in construction of the heap, turning of material, and maintenance of adequate moisture. Loss of nitrogen as ammonia gas also takes place, which can be considerably reduced. Economy is use of water is also possible if composting is carried out in pits instead of heaps.

Bangalore Method

This method was worked out, firstly to overcome some of the disadvantages of the Indore method, and secondly to process night soil and city refuse. In fact, before the method was developed, the disposal of night soil collected for dry latrines in Indian towns was a real problem. Although, it was known as an anaerobic method, in reality, it is aerobic to start with, followed by anaerobic decomposition later. This method is also known as hot fermentation method, as heat loss during decomposition is considerably reduced (Acharya 1939, 1940). Though initially worked out for towns, it can be used for compost-making from conveniently available organic materials. Under rural conditions, animal dung can be used to substitute night soil, for night soil is generally not collected in rural areas.

To carry out composting by the Bangalore method, trenches of about 1 m depth, 1.5 - 2.5m width, and of any length are made at an appropriate place, generally on the outskirts of the city. If material is limited, one can go in for pits of 1 m depth, 1.5 m width, and 3 - 4 m length. The compostable refuse is dumped into the trench or pit and spread out with rakes or forked shovels to make a layer of about 1.5 cm thickness. Night soil or dung is then placed over the refuse in a layer of about 5 cm. The process is repeated until the trench or pit is filled up to about 30 cm above the ground level and a final layer of compostable material is placed on the top. At each layering, water is sprinkled over the material to make it optimally moist. The above-ground material is made into a dome shape and covered with about 2.5 cm mud-plaster. If all operations are properly carried out, the compost is ready in about five to six months, a period of about one-and-a-half time longer than that for aerobic composting by the Indore method.

Modifications

Modifications of the original methods of composting have been attempted at one place or the other, from time to time, in order to speed up the process. It should be remembered that rapid composting conserves more nutrients of the compost materials than slow composting carried out at leisure. The Chinese high temperature composting method is a combination of the aerobic and anaerobic methods (RAPA, 1988). To make the so-called high temperature compost, after the heap is erected, hollow bamboo pipes are inserted into it both vertically and horizontally. In two to three days, the temperature of the heap rises to 60-70°C. The poles are then removed and the heap is plastered with mud. The plaster is broken after 15 days and the heap is turned thoroughly. If need be, moisture is adjusted to appropriate levels. The heap is replastered and left for natural decomposition. The compost will be ready in about two months, whereas it takes about four months by the ordinary aerobic method.

Some quicker aerobic composting methods have been suggested (Rodale 1960). Quick intermittent turning of the material is the cardinal point of these methods. These are modifications of the Indore method. With the provisions of adequate moisture, the compost heap is turned thoroughly at three-day intervals. This way, a fairly good compost is ready for use in about three weeks

Factors affecting the Process of Composting

The waste degradation and quality of compost depends on the following abiotic and biotic factors:

Abiotic Factors

1. Chemical Nature of Raw Materials

The carbonaceous compounds in the plant residues are cellulose hemicellulose and lignin. Protein constituents like cellulose and hemicellulose decompose easily, lignin is resistant to microbial attack to a considerable extent. Hence, raw material for composting should be predominantly of cellulose nature. At the same time, lignin also suffers slow degradation following the flush of cellulose degradation.

2. Carbon and Nitrogen Ratio

The abundance of carbon and protein in organic matter and the carbon : nitrogen ratio play a very significant role in microbial food supply. Generally C : N ratios ranging from 30 to 50 have been used for composting. (Gaur 1984)

3. Moisture

Moisture content of 60-70% is generally considered optimum to start with. At later stages of decomposition, it may be 50 - 60%. Provision of optimum moisture in the substrate material is essential for the metabolism of micro-organisms. Excess moisture creates anaerobic conditions in the heap and brings about putrefaction. Putrefaction produces disagreeable odours and undesirable products. Also excess of moisture inhibit aerobic microbial activity.

4. Aeration

Aeration controls the internal environment of the compost heaps. It regulates the microbial activity. Less aeration creates anaerobic condition. In all traditional methods, good aeration is achieved by giving frequent turnings to the material.

5. Temperature

In the aerobic system, the temperature rises to 50 - 60°C in just few days and goes even upto 700C in two to three weeks. The high temperature destroys weed seeds, pathogenic micro-organisms, maggots and worms and prevents fly breeding.

6. Reaction or pH

The optimum pH of most microorganisms is between 6.5 - 7.5. Organic acids are produced at the time of decomposition but their existence is only transitory. So if the material has undergone putrefaction anaerobic decomposition takes place and appreciable amounts of troublesome organic acids are produced. In such a situation addition of materials like lime or wood ash helps in neutralizing excessive acidity.

Biotic Factors

Microbial pattern in composting systems

The compostable organic materials are naturally inhabited by large number of heterotrophic microbes. This is in correspondence which bring about satisfactory decomposition under appropriate environmental conditions. Maximum increase in microbial numbers in notice in first one or two weeks of incubation and maximum $C^{o}2$ evolution is observed during the same period. Although bacteria are in greater abundance than fungi in soil, in studies on the natural decomposition of organic materials, fungal flora has received greater attention. Being efficient consumers of carbon and proportionate amount of nitrogen, fungi build up much higher biomass than other micro-organisms.

THE 'DO-HOW' OF VERMICOMPOSTING

As described earlier, the degradation of organic waste by earthwormic consumption is known as Vermicomposting. The process of vermicomposting is shown in the flow sheet Figure. 6.1. Basically, there are three phases in the process of Vermicomposting:

Phase I

Collection of the waste; separation of metal, glass, ceramics etc., from the organic waste; storage of the organic waste.

Phase II

Earthworm beds are maintained and the earthworms are 'fed' with the organic waste.

Phase III

After the organic waste has been worked over by the earthworms, the vermicompost, the cocoons, the earthworms and the uningested materials are separated.

There are several 'Vermicomposting packages' being developed, varying in the design and construction of the vermicomposting pits, the species of earthworms used, the nature of the feed material, the bedding material for the earthworms and so on.

What is obtained from the whole process of vermicomposting is:

(i) The treatment and disposal of selected biodegradable

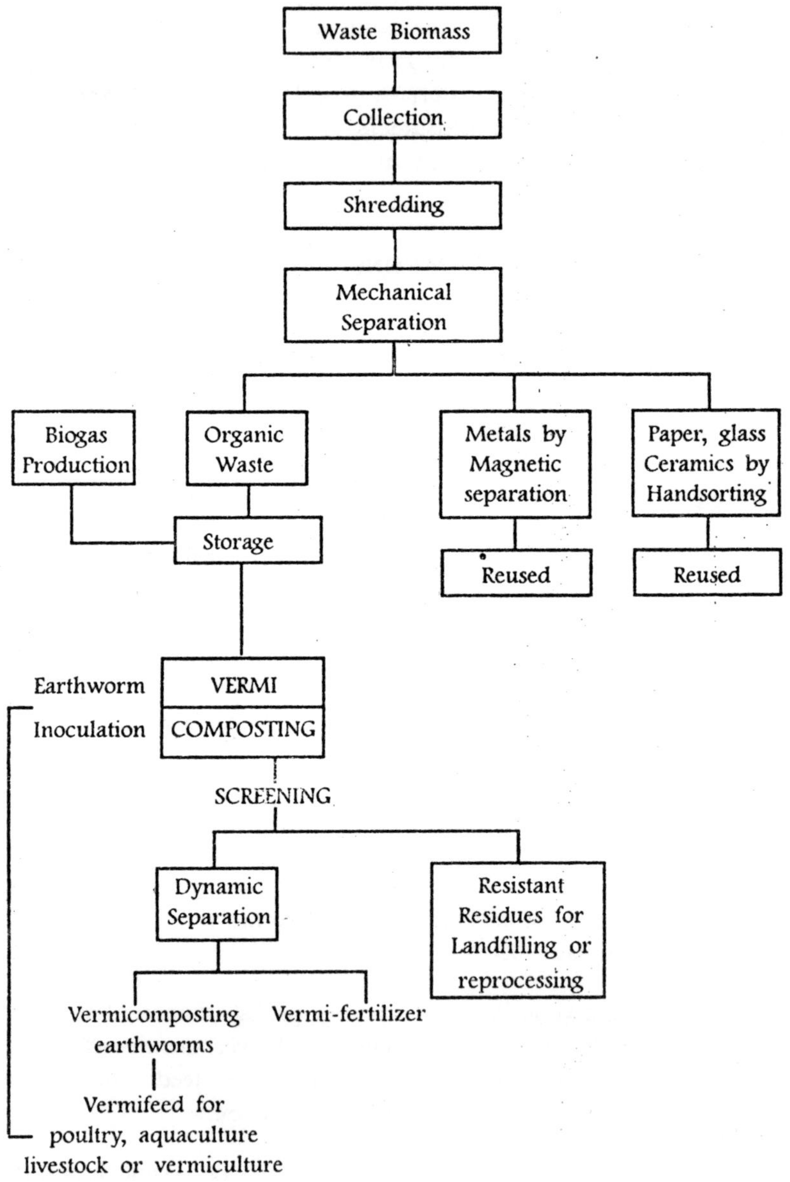

Figure 6.1 Vermicomposting flow sheet

waste; in otherwords those waste substances that are suitable for earthwormic consumption can be processed and disposed of. Thus it aids in the abatement of organic pollution by reduction in wastes bulk density and elimination of foul odour.

(ii) An end product of the process is vermicompost, which is nothing but the castings of the earthworms. This vermicompost is rich in plant nutrients.

(iii) One of the by-products is vermiwash, which is now being tapped. To put it simply, it is a solution of nutrients, obtained from the percolation of water through the vermi-castings. A simple technique for the production and collection of vermiwash has been described later on in this chapter.

(iv) Another by-product is the earthworms themselves. They are found to be very good sources of protein. The production of vermiprotein in the form of earthworms, can be used as animal feed.

If one wants to compare vermicomposting with composting, a few observations can be made

Vermicomposting	Composting
* Prior size reduction is not needed.	Proper shredding of the waste is needed to increase the surface area of microbial action.
* By their burrowing action, earthworms aerate the systems therefore, turning is not needed.	The waste needs to be turned over to aerate the system.
* Earthworms secrete mucus, which helps in maintaining favourable pH 6.5 to 7.5.	
* The wormcasts which are aggregates, helps in aeration.	There is no formation of substantial aggregation.
* The end products are vermicompost, protein supplement in the form of worm tissue, vermiwash.	The end product is compost.

* There is no malodour	Proper conditions have to be maintained for prevention of malodour.
* The time taken for the conversion of the waste is relatively lesser.	The time taken is relatively more
* The same piece of land can be used continuously & for more harvests of the compost.	Since the time taken for composting is quite long, the plot can be reused only after the process of composting is completed.
* The vermicomposting pits in some cases have to have protection against heavy rainfall, direct sunlight, predators.	

VERMICOMPOST

Soil entering the mouth of the earthworms is processed and then excreted through the anus in the form of compact, concentrated mass known as vermicastings. Vermicastings are a highly enriched kind of biofertilizer. It is more chemically neutral than the surrounding soil. Earthworm casts contain more micro-organisms, inorganic minerals and organic matter in the form available to plants. Casts also contain enzymes such as proteases, amylases, lipases, cellulases and chitinases; which continue to disintegrate organic matter even after they have been excreted. Comparison of vermicasts with the surrounding soils have invariably indicated that casts have a higher base-exchange capacity and are generally richer in total organic matter, total exchangeable bases, available phosphorus, exchangeable potassium and manganese, and total and exchangeable calcium. The nutrient value of worm castings is not high compared to chemical fertilizers. The key factor is microbial activity. Microbial activity is 10-20 times higher than in the soil and organic matter that the worm ingests. The most important effect of earthworms may be the stimulation of microbial activity that occurs in casts. This enhances the transformation of soluble nitrogen into microbial protein; preventing their loss by leaching to the lower horizons of the soil.

The beneficial influence of worm cast has been related to the biological factors like gibberellin, cytokinins and auxins released due to microbial activity of the microbes harboured in the cast. There are reports that certain metabolites produced by earthworms may be responsible for stimulating plant growth. It is considered that earthworms release into the soil certain vitamins and similar substances which may be B group vitamins or some provitamin D or free amino acids. The amount of vitamin B_{12} is generally known to increase two-fold within an year or two after the introduction of worms. Though the NPK value of the vermicast is always lower than any standard chemical fertilizer, several experiments have proved that wormcasts can promote lush growth of plants which probably may be due to plant growth promoters like cytokinins and auxins present in the casts. Presence of compounds allied to Indole Acetic acid in the earthworm tissues has been demonstrated in the earthworm tissues. The antibacterial activity of coelomic fluid of earthworms is accounted and this activity is only directed against the highly pathogenic soil bacteria. So from these available information, it could be deduced that earthworms apart from encouraging the establishment of beneficial micro-organisms to some extent, can also inhibit the soil borne pathogens.

Vermicompost is better than chemical fertilizers in economical and ecological aspects. Replacing costly yet deadly chemicals with cheap yet friendly vermicompost will ensure sustainable food production.

Use of vermicompost as manure has multifolded benefits. They are:

1) Healthy soil with soil organisms;
2) Limited external inputs;
3) Cost effective farming practices and healthy food;
4) Problems of leaching and mineralization of nutrients are reduced.

Vermicompost as Carrier for Biofertilisers

Vermicompost is one such material which is being experimented as a growth media and carried for biofertilizers. A carrier should be able to sustain viable growth of atleast 10^6 to 10^8 cells of bacteria. The final physical structure of the plant growth media or vermicompost produced from organic wastes depends very much on the original material from which they are produced. The final product is usually a finely divided peat like material with excellent structure, porosity, drainage and moisture holding capacity. Since vermicompost contains high levels of nitrogen, phosphates, potassium, carbon and organic matter all of which are essential for the growth of microbes. This property of vermicompost makes it an ideal medium for growth of microbial populations. The application of organics helps the microorganisms to produce polysaccharides; nitrogen fixation and phosphorus solubilization due to improved microbiological activity. Vermicompost is rich in digested organic matter, thus providing a good substrate for growth of microorganisms. During the processing of wastes by earthworms many of the nutrients they contain are changed to more readily available forms such as nitrates, exchangeable phosphorus and soluble potassium, calcium and magnesium. The water holding capacity of vermicompost is high. (Lalitha 1997).

EARTHWORM AND PROTEIN PRODUCTION

Going by the protein content of earthworms, for example, *Lumbricus terrestris* is reported to contain 66.25 % protein, *Aporrectodea longa* 68.12 %. *Octolasion cyaneum* 60% and *Eisenia foetida* 60-61 % (Lee 1985) and in terms of its nutritious quality, earthworm protein being valued as equally nutritious as fish meal or meat meal (Veeresh 1984).

Sâbine (1978) and Yoshida and Hoshii (1978) have suggested that the possible substitution of earthworms as protein substitute in feed of pigs and poultry respectively. Arunachalam and Palanichamy (1984) have shown the improved growth rate of fish *Mystus Villatus* when fed on either dry or fresh worms. Dash et al, 1977; Dash and Senapati (1985) have reported high protein, nitrogen and fat content in *Lampitto mauritii*, a widely occurring worm in India. Guerro (1981) has reported a protein value of 54.77 and fat of 13.35% in *Perionyx excavatus*. Table 6.1 shows the amino acid composition

% of high protein supplements and Table 6.2 shows the amino acid composition of worm meals and fish meals. Considering the fact that the earthworms on average, can convert 20-40 % of their assimilated energy into high quality protein rich in most of the essential amino acids (Senapati, 1992). and going by the feeding trials in which growth, food consumption and efficiency of food conversion were estimated, the potential of earthworm meal as a protein source in the diet of broilers was reported by Reinecke et al.(1991), and the feeding trials of Japanese quails and broilers by Das and Dash (1989) Table 6.3 depicts quail growth analysis 8-56 days. Table 6.4 denotes chicken growth analysis 7-52 days. and also that poultry feed production is expected to increase to 56 x 10^6 tons by the end of the decade from a production of 2.989 x O^6 tons in 1984, one can see the potential of earthworm meal as a protein supplement.

TABLE—6.1

Amino acid composition (%) of high-protein supplements (Sabine, 1981)

	Worm meal	*Meat meal*	*Fish meal*
Arginine	4.13	3.48	3.9
Cystine	2.29	1.07	0.8
Glutamic acid	—	—	8.4
Glycine	2.92	7.09	4.4
Histidine	1.56	0.97	1.5
Lsoleucine	2.58	1.33	3.6
Leucine	4.84	3.54	5.1
Lysine	4.33	3.08	6.4
Methionine	2.18	1.45	1.8
Phonylalanine	2.25	2.17	2.6
Serine	2.88	2.15	—
Threonine	2.95	1.77	2.8
Tryptophan	—	—	0.7
Tyrosine	1.36	1.29	1.8
Valine	3.01	2.22	3.5
Crude protein	61.0	51.0	60.9

Source : Senapathi, B.K., 1992.

TABLE—6.2

Amino acid composition of worm meals and fish meals

	Eisenia fetida	*Eudrilus eugeniae*	*Perionyx excavatus*	*Fish meal*	*Broiler starter*	*Lumbricus* terristris*	*Allolophobra* longa*
Aspartic acid						9.35	11.35
Threonine	4.47	4.30	4.20	3.84	3.33	5.12	4.8
Serine	4.44	4.50	4.61	14.30	4.12	5.47	2.4
Valine	6.00	5.95	5.88	5.00	3.95	4.75	5.6
Methionine	1.80	1.75	1.90	2.66	2.08	2.29	1.14
Isoleucine	4.60	4.58	4.55	4.06	3.58	4.53	5.10
Leucine	9.80	9.60	9.85	7.80	6.42	8.48	8.13
Tyrosine	3.50	2.95	3.14	3.69	2.87	4.17	6.04
Phenylanine	3.58	3.02	3.62	3.08	3.30	4.17	6.04
Histidine	3.37	3.10	3.22	2.23	0.19	2.85	2.30
Lysine	7.76	7.85	7.80	7.15	4.99	7.26	7.81
Arginine	9.56	9.20	9.33	4.62	6.24	6.54	7.17
Glutamic acid*	17.70	13.80				17.56	13.66
Alanine*	6.50	5.20				6.03	5.97
Cystine*	6.70	1.60				0.66	0.68
% Protein	66.13	58.38	61.63	61.00	22.0	—	—

Source: Reinecke, Hayes and Cilliers, 1990.
* Veeresh, 1984.

For protein production, the waste has to be inoculated with cocoons for young ones and for compost production adult worms which can maximise the output of the waste. Figure 6.2 shows the worm populations for protein production and compost production. To maintain maximum biomass production and the stocking rate of 1:10 in terms of biomass of worms to biomass of waste gives maximum biomass productivity in most of the organic wastes as shown in Figure 6.3. Alawdeen and Ismail (1986) suggest that the fairly high content of protein and minerals and low concentration of fat renders the non-cillates of *Lampito mauritii* preferable for consumption. But before one can start thinking of worm meal as the answer for protein supplement, there are number of problems associated with earthworm protein production. Earthworm serve as secondary or intermediate hosts to common mammalian and avian pathogens, such as *Histomonas spp*, a protozoan parasite that causes blackhead in fowls . Hence it may be necessary to sterilize the vermiprotein. The pathogens harboured by the earthworm may be harmful to humans, so posing potential problems using earthworm meal as pet food or vermicast for plants in domestic environment. If the earthworms have accumulated hazardous substances like heavy metals, the meal procured from the earthworm is not safe, so the nature and safety of the feeding material has to be ensured. There may be economic problems in that production of vermiprotein may not be feasible economically.

TABLE—6.3

Quail Growth Analysis Days 8.56 (inclusive)

	Fish meal ration (C)	*Earthworm meal ration(T)*
Mean weight gain (g)	96.1	98.5
Feed consumption (g)	533.0	511.0
Feed conversion ratio	5.54	5.19
Mean rate of growth (g/day)	1.96	2.01

Source : Das, A.K. and Dash M.C., 1989.

Table 6.4

Chicken growth analysis, day 7-52

	Fish meal ration	*Earthworm meal ration*
Mean weight gain (kg)	1.117	1.171
Feed consumption (kg chicken-1, 46 days)	2.528	2.523
Feed conversion ratio	2.263	2.154
Mean rate of growth (kg day-1)	0.024	0.025

Source : Das, A.K. and Dash M.C., 1989.

As such vermiprotein or vermimeal is considered as the bonus from the vermicomposting process.

Vermiwash

Technologists at the Yusuf Meherally Centre, Pannel Maharashtra, have developed a simple method to extract the vermiwash, yielding

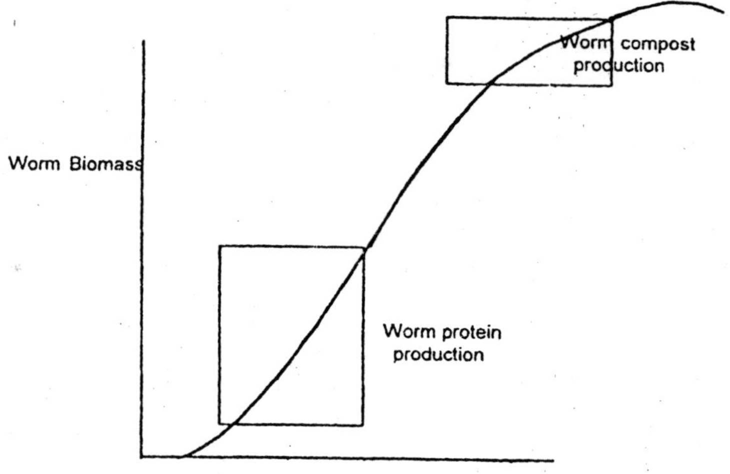

Figure 6.2 Worm populations for protein production and compost production
(*Source* : Edwards and Burrows, 1985)

about 1.5 liters of vermiwash a day. Figure 6.4 shows simplified diagram of the system. The system consists of 100 litre plastic barrel, in which a perforated plastic waste paper basket is placed at the centre, upside down, a central 1mt plastic tube 5 cms wide with hole upto 7.5 cms height at the dipped end . Around the waste paper basket is placed broken bricks and packed sand upto 7.5 cms deep. The plastic pipe should pass through the center of the waste paper basket, such that the end of the holes touches the base of the barrel. The whole assembly is kept inside the thatched shed or any cool corner of a farm shed. Above the mixed brick and sand, comes a layer of humus, along with about 5000 earthworms. Everyday, 2 to 3 tablespoons of fresh cowdung slurry is spread over the humus layer, and/or vegetable waste, fruit peels etc as feed for the earthworms. Also about 2 litres of water is poured from the top. The water percolates down and collects at the bottom of the plastic barrel, this water brings along with part of the casts of the earthworms as vermiwash, which can be siphoned from the barrel. The vermiwash can be applied to the root zone of plants , or diluted 4 times then sprayed over the foliage, and may be added to compost pits, to hasten the degradation process.

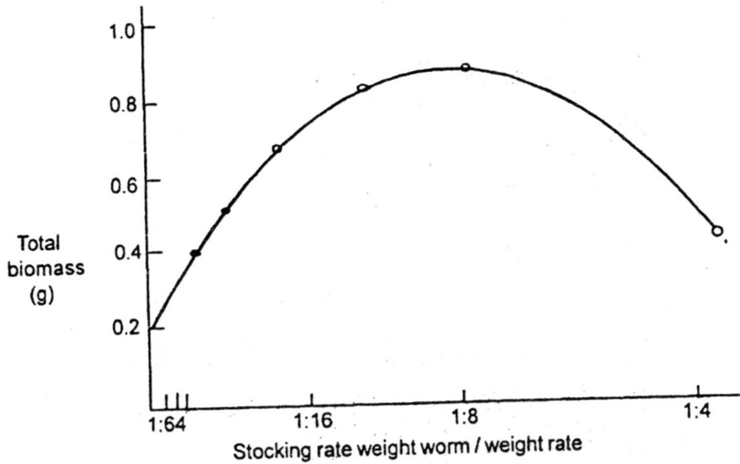

Figure. 6.3 Stocking rates with Elsenia foetida for maximum biomass production.
(*Source* : Edwards and Burrows, 1985)

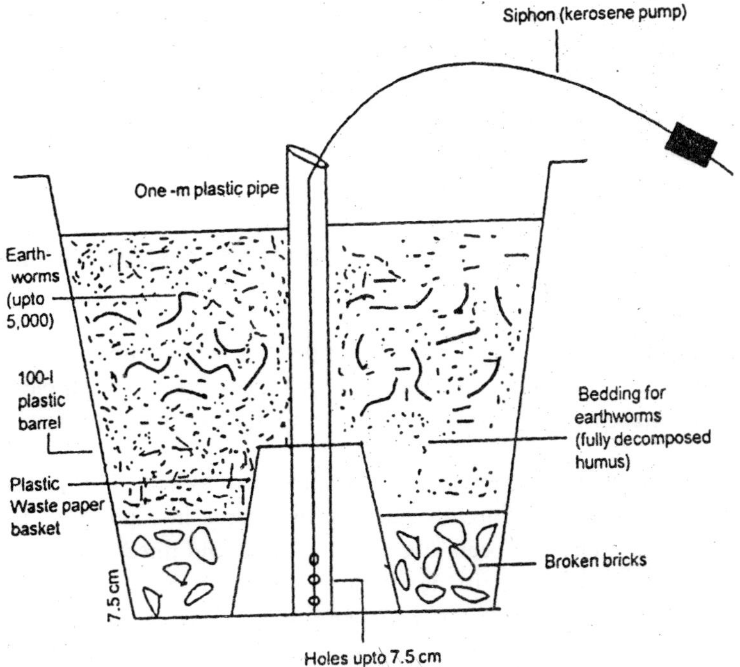

Figure. 6.4 Extraction of vermiwash

7

VERMICOMPOSTING SYSTEMS

K. Senthilvelan*

Vermicomposting may be carried out at different scales and with different objectives—for a household, a community, or a city; and for just disposing solid waste to run a commercial enterprise. Accordingly different types of vermicomposting systems are in use across India. A few illustrative examples are given in this chapter. The information is based on the details kindly provided to us on request by the scientists working in these institutions.

THE G.B. PANT INSTITUTE OF HIMALAYAN ENVIRONMENT DEVELOPMENT

The Institute has tried weed composting with common crop field weeds and Banmara (*Eupatorium adenophorum*), to supplement traditional cowdung manure, in an attempt to control weed infestation.

The process consists of chopping the collected weeds into manageable size and tightly packing the weeds into pits (1.2 x 1.2 x 1.2m) which have been dug in the ground and lined with coconut jute. The weeds are moistened with water and the pit is then covered with a bamboo frame or polythene sheet, leaving atleast 0.5 m

* Er. K. Senthilvelan, M.E, Ph.D is a Scientist with Centre for Pollution Control and Energy Technology.

clearance from the top of the heap, to prevent rainwater infiltration. In the first 3-4 days, the temperature within the pit begins to rise and continues to be higher than the ambient temperature for about 15 days, then the temperature starts to decline. Once the temperature has become normal, the earthworms are introduced into the pit. After the conversion of the decomposed weeds into worm castings, the castings are harvested.

DR. ISMAIL, DIRECTOR, INSTITUTE OF RESEARCH IN SOIL BIOLOGY & BIOTECHNOLOGY, THE NEW COLLEGE, CHENNAI

He has come out with a system, starting from the construction of the compost pit to the harvesting of the vermicompost.

Compost pit

The compost pit can be dug in the ground, or constructed with brick and mortar. It can be of any convenient size. An easily manageable pit size seems to be 2m x 1m x 1m.

Vermibed

The bottom of the compost pit is filled with approximately 15-20 cm high layer of a good loamy soil. This soil layer is called the vermibed and is the 'home' of the earthworms. This vermibed is kept moist but never flooded.

Inoculation of earthworms

About 100 local adult earthworms can be accomodated in a pit size of 2 x 1 x 1m.

Dry layering

Next, lumps of fresh cattle dung are randomly strewn over the vermibed. Then some dry leaves or hay, to about 6 cm is placed over the vermibed. The compost pit is kept moist by watering for about 30 days. During this period, the pit may be covered with leaves of coconut or palmyra.

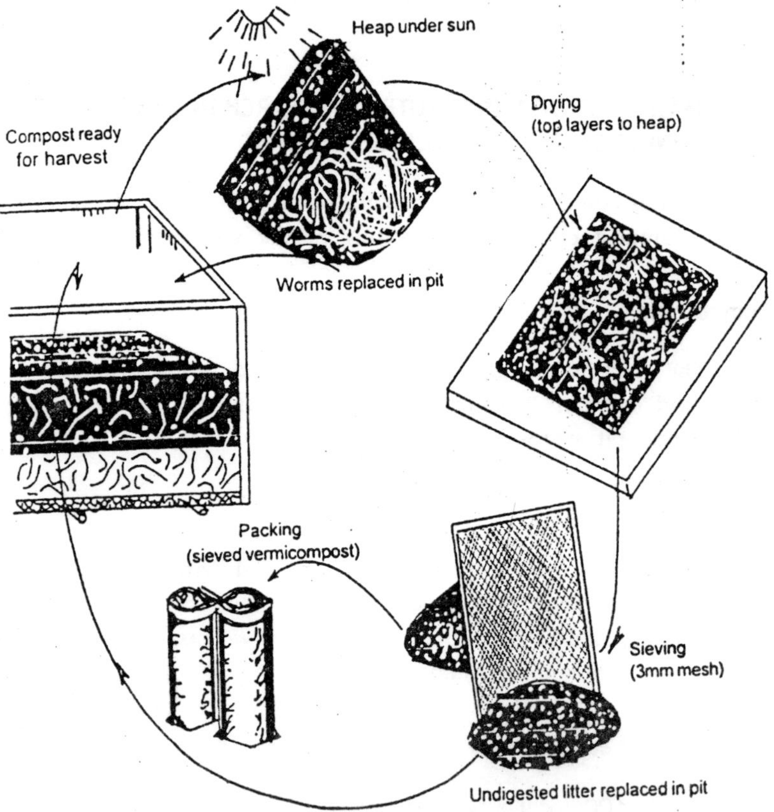

Fig, 7.1. Stages of harvesting of Vermicompost
(Source : Ismail et al, 1993)

Wet layering

After the period of 30 days of dry layering, wet organic waste from the kitchen or hotel or hostel or farm can be spread over the dry layer to a maximum height of 5 cms. Depending upon the rate of consumption of the wet organic matter by the earthworms, the input of the organic matter can be repeated say twice a week.

The organic waste can be turned over and mixed periodically, taking care not to disturb the vermibed. The addition of the wet organic waste is continued week after week, till the pit is full. Once the pit is full, it is kept moist for another 30 to 45 days and the contents are turned over carefully. Moistening of the pit should cease 3 to 4 days prior to harvesting, thus allowing the compost to dry and the earthworms to retreat to their vermibed.

Harvesting

The compost is dug out and then dried, then sieved through 2 mm sieve, to separate the cocoons, earthworms and undecomposed and uningested material. The sieved compost is further dried and packed for use. The cocoons and juveniles and adult earthworms are replaced into the pit or used to start a fresh culture. Table 7.1 gives an estimation of the production capacity, the economics of the vermicomposting system and Table 7.2 gives a time table for the vermicomposting process. Figure 7.1 illustrates the formation of the vermibed and vermicompost by Dr. Ismail, New College, Madras.

TABLE—7.1
Vermitech and its economics

Construction and Maintenance of a Twin Unit		
Production Capacity		
Total Surface area for production (2m x 1m x 1m per unit)	$2\ m^2 \times 2$ =	$4\ m^2$
Annual targeted production capacity	1500 Kg x 2	= 3000 Kg
Duration of each run (average/unit)	=	120 days
Number of harvests of compost per year	3/unit x 2 =	6 (approx)

FEASIBILITY REPORT

Estimated Capital Investment

Vermitech Units		
Brick and mortar		
with shade made of sheets	=	Rs. 13,500.00
Vermibed	=	Rs. 500.00
Implements	=	Rs. 500.00
Contingencies	=	Rs. 500.00
TOTAL	=	Rs. 15,000.00

(a) Fixed Cost		
(i) Depreciation @ 10 %	=	Rs. 1500.00
(ii) Interest @ 15%	=	Rs. 1800.00
TOTAL		Rs. 3300.00

Total fixed costs approximately Rs.3,500.00 only

(b) Variable Costs		
(i) Cost of inputs @ Rs.200/produce	=	Rs. 1200.00
(ii) Labour 2hr/day @ Rs.9/hr	=	Rs. 825.00
(iii) Harvesting and packing @ Rs.150/harvest	=	Rs. 600.00
		Rs. 2625.00

Total variable cost approximately Rs.3,000.00 only

COST RETURN ANALYSIS

1.	Total Cultivable space	=	4 m^2 (2m^2 + 2 m^2)
2.	Estimated production (minimum)	=	3000 kg
3.	Revenue from sale proceeds (@ Rs.5/- per kg)	=	Rs. 15000/-
4.	Total fixed cost	=	Rs. 3500/-
5.	Total variable cost	=	Rs. 3000/-
6.	Total cost (4 + 5)	=	Rs. 6500/-
7.	Profit (3-6)	=	Rs. 8500/-
8.	Total capital investment	=	Rs. 15000/-
9.	Pay Back Period (8/7)	=	1.76 Year(say 2 years)
10.	Cost of Production per Kg (6/2) (Say Re. 1.00 only per Kg)	=	Rs. 2.16(say, Rs 2.25)

(Ismail, 1997)

TABLE—7.2

Effective time table for proper harvesting of vermicompost using geophytophagous anecic earthworms. (Twin unit system)

	Day		*Unit 1*		*Unit 2*
FIRST YEAR	0		Vermibed		————
	30		Start loading		————
	45		————		Vermibed
	75		Stop loading		Begin loading
	120	(1)	Harvest and cure		————
	125		Reload		Stop loading
	165		————	(2)	Harvest and cure
	170		Stop		Reload
	215	(3)	Harvest and cure		————
	220		Reload		Stop
	265		————	(4)	Harvest and cure
	270		Stop		Relaod
	315	(5)	Harvest and cure		————
	320		Reload		Stop
	365		————	(6)	Harvest and cure
SECOND YEAR	370		Stop		Reload
	415	(7)	Harvest cure		————
	420		Reload		Stop
	465		————	(8)	Harvest and cure
	470		Stop		Reload
	515	(9)	Harvest cure		————
	520		Reload		Stop
	565		————	(10)	Harvest and cure
	570		Stop		Reload
	615	(11)	Harvest cure		————
	620		Reload		Stop
	665		————	(12)	Harvest and cure
	670		Stop		Reload
	715	(13)	Harvest cure		————
	720		Reload		Stop

(Ismail 1997)

INORA: INSTITUTE OF NATURAL ORGANIC AGRICULTURE

INORA has developed a process for what it calls as industrial wormi-composting of waste. The INORA process has five units:

Unit 1

Assuming that the waste collected is organic in nature, it is shredded, using a shredding machine to a few millimetre particle size.

Unit 2

This is the Bio-sanitization unit. The shredded waste from unit 1 is recieved by a conveyer belt or manually and piled into heaps of about 4 x 4 x 4 ft. The heaps are well aerated and inoculated with micro-organisms and moistened with water, the water can be obtained from the biogas sludge of Unit 3 or the water that is extracted in the shredding process. The end product is a pulpy material.

Unit 3

This consists of the Bio-gas process. Here, the biogas plant receives the bio-sanitized material in a mixing chamber, to which fresh cowdung in the ratio of 50:25 is also mixed in. Human excreta is also piped into the biogas plant. Further mixing is carried out by a fan or manually. After the retention time, the gas is collected in balloons and the dewatered sludge effluent is put in use in the next unit.

Unit 4

This unit consists of the Wormi-Composting Process. This process takes place in sheds of a special design. Part of the bio-sanitized material of unit 2 is laid in heaps of size 50 x 3.5 x 1.5 ft. Each shed contains 2 or 4 of such heaps in long rows. Each row is innoculated with about 20,000 worms. The organic material from unit 2 and unit 3 are laid layer by layer in the heap, followed by a layer of cooled cowdung. The heap is then covered by a jute cloth. Watering is done over the jute cloth. Temperature and moisture levels are maintained at around 25°-28°C and 30-35% respectively.

The heaps are aerated through pipes at the bottom of the heaps. Initially, under the optimum conditions of temperature, moisture and aeration, the wormicompost is said to be ready in about 40 days and this period is brought down, as the earthworm population increases. When the wormicompost is ready for harvesting, watering of the heaps is stopped 2-3 days before hand. The compost material is piled into pyramidal forms, the earthworms then go to the lower layers of the compost material, then the upper layers of the compost material is removed and then sieved. In this way, there is separation of the wormi-compost.

Unit 5

This consists of secondary sorting and adjusting of the wormicompost to meet the demands of the market.

CENTRE FOR ENVIRONMENTAL EDUCATION CEE SOUTHERN REGIONAL CELL, BANGALORE

Wastes are segregated into four categories namely, dry, wet, toxic and soiled wastes.

Dry waste

This consists of scraps of paper, plastic, metal, glass pieces, rags, rubber, leather and crockery. The dry wastes are collected by the trainee ragpicker. Wicker baskets have been provided to encourage the separation of the dry wastes.

Wet Waste

This is made up of the kitchen wastes like vegetable and fruit peels, garden litter. This is the waste that can be composted and are collected by the trainee ragpicker. Plastic bins have been provided to store these wet wastes.

Toxic waste

Materials such as leftover pesticides, expired medicines, used batteries, left over paints etc. are to be tied in a bag and left for the corporation to dispose of it.

Soiled waste

Soiled and infected cotton, drips, injection syringes, diapers, needles, sanitary napkins. These wastes are to be tied in bags and left in corporation bins for disposal.

The cell has selected four ragpicker boys. These boys are being trained, so as to be able to manage the whole scheme on their own, in the near future. The trainees are given uniforms, protective footwear, gloves. They collect the segregated waste from the residents in tricycles which have been acquired with the help of State Bank of India. The compostable wastes are brought to vermicomposting pits in Coles Park. Further the trainees are paid, they are given breakfast, medical care and they undergo a literary programme. Surprisingly the municipal corporation has been supportive to the whole scheme and has infact allowed the construction of the vermicomposting pits is Coles Park free of charge. The pits, have been made from mortar, have protective meshing and sloping roofs. They measure 6 x 4 x 2 ft. The cost of each pit was approximately Rs. 8000/-, though rather expensive, the location of the pits was kept in mind, being in a public park, there are high possibilities of vandalism. The following Table 7.3 gives an idea of the cost of a scheme/venture of a clean neighbourhood.

As such, the programme focusses on awareness of a clean environment, the role an individual can play which can significantly be reflected in the cleanliness of the neighbourhood, on the possibilities of treating/disposing of ones own waste in house.

IIT MADRAS

It has formed a voluntary group, known as "SWARM GROUP", to deal with solid waste management. They are processing their campus waste through vermiculture technique, suggested by Dr. Ismail of New College, Madras and Prof. Sarkar, IIT, Bombay.

The pit is of size 2m x 1m x 1m lined with broken bricks of size upto 25 mm and covered with a layer of river sand to a height of 100 mm. Above the sand layer, loamy (fertile) soil is added to a height of about 150 mm and moistened with water. Next, after the layering, fresh cowdung and leaf litter is strewn over the loamy soil. This forms the vermibed to house the earthworms.

TABLE—7.3
Expenses/month of the CEE scheme

Sl.No.	*Particulars*	*Expenses/month*
1.	Salary of ragpickers=4 x 500	2000
2.	Salary of Supervisor	1500
3.	Rent for housing the tricycles	200
4.	Maintenance	500
5.	Breakfast for Trainees	900
6.	Contingency 15 %	785
	Total	5885

About 150 earthworms collected locally are introduced into the bed. After feeding on the cowdung and leaf litter in 40% moisture condition, the earthworms are fed on organic waste such as kitchen waste every alternate day. The moisture condition of the pit is maintained at 40%. Once the pit is full, the addition of waste is ceased and the contents are turned over. A thin layer of soil is spread over and the 40% moisture condition is still maintained. The covered pit is kept so for about 30 days. At the end of this period, the waste material should have been worked upon by the earthworms. The worm worked material is removed from the pit and piled in heaps. The earthworms move to the bottom of the heap. The top layers are removed, dried and then sieved. The vermicompost is reported to contain 2.2% of nitrogen, 1.8% of phosphorous and traces of potassium. According to Dr.Swaminathan of SWARM, problems such as flooding of the vermicomposting pits can be dealt with, such as choosing a well draining soil type in the location of the composting pit or by providing roofing over the pit.

Dr. Swaminathan remarked that on a supposedly organised campus such as that of IIT, Madras, if one finds it difficult to get the waste segregated at the source itself, (this making more sense than segregation of the collective waste at the common point), then the application of vermicomposting in other situations may face difficulty.

EXNORA INTERNATIONAL MADRAS

Solid waste management is one of the issues handled by Exnora International, Madras. The members are asked to segregate their wastes into organics and dry waste consisting of paper, plastics, glass etc. These wastes are collected from door to door by individuals hired by the organisation. The organic waste is deposited neatly into municipal dustbins and the dry waste sold to waste retailers for recycling. Presently, a further step towards solid waste management is being taken, the residents are being asked to compost the organic, compostable wastes at the household level itself, if there is enough space for a composting pit to be dug or cement or plastic composting containers to be maintained. If it is not possible to vermicompost the waste in situ, Exnora has plans to have vermicomposting pits on a fairly large scale, so as to carry out the process at the community level. It is hoped that the compostable waste will be brought to the community vermicomposting pits, measuring 20x6x4 ft. Exnora has tried to involve the Narikoravas in the scheme, by hiring them to collect the wasfe and deposit the waste. Each individual is paid about Rs.600 per month, in addition to his income acquired by the selling of the recyclable waste collected from his quota of residential homes. The organization has consulted Dr.Ismail, New College, Madras on the technical issues of the vermicomposting process.

DR.L. VENKATARATNAM, CHAIRMAN, AGRI-HORTICULTURAL SOCIETY, PUBLIC GARDENS, HYDERABAD

The garbage is segregated to obtain the bio-degradable organic waste, manually. This waste is then shredded by a motorized chaff-cutter. Cow dung slurry is added with the shredded garbage. The shredded garbage, charged with cow dung slurry is then heaped in 24 rows of 2 feet height and 5 feet width and sprinkled with water for 3-4 hours daily. Then the garbage is placed on beds of straw of about 50 cms in height under thatched sheds. The humidity is maintained at around 30 %, the pH is maintained around 6.5 and temperature is not to exceed 28°C. About 200 locally harvested earthworms are inoculated into the garbage. The garbage is worked upon by microbes and earthworms in about two months time.

Watering is stopped two days prior to harvesting. The earthworm worked garbage is then heaped, allowing the earthworms to settle at the bottom of the heap and the vermicompost is harvested, dried and sieved and ready for use. Table 7.4 shows the estimated budget for a pilot project for vermicomposting.

YASHPAL SUHAG'S EARTHWORM BREEDING CENTRE (NORTH DELHI)

A massive breeding centre for earthworms has come up in North Delhi. Brainchild of a young, educated farmer, the centre has more than 15 million of worms turning biodegradable wastes into manure.

Mr. Yashpal Suhag, who has set up the project at a 1.5 acre farmhouse in Narela, claims he can turn the city's bio-degradable garbage of all kinds, human excreta, cow dung, fallen leaves and other such wastes, into manure. Such a proposal was made by him to the Delhi Government.

Whether or not the Delhi Government employs Mr. Suhag's services, it is taking earthworm culture seriously. It plans to introduce earthworm-filled baskets in primary and secondary schools to be used as "environment-friendly dustbins." The waste will become fine manure within days.

Mr. Suhag's success story began two years ago when he purchased 30,000 earthworms from Bhawalkar's Earthworms Research Institute (BERI) Pune, which encourages farmers to take up organic farming. He says a tonne of waste can be turned into manure within a fortnight by using about 1,000 earthworms. The worms multiply at a fairly rapid pace. A pair produces about 250 offsprings in a year.

Mr. Suhag has been imparting training in earthworm culture to 35 unemployed youth and farmers in past few months. He says the awareness about the earthworm's utility was spreading fast among farmers in several states. According to him, farmers at Varanasi, Pantnagar, Nainital, Rudrapur(UP), Samalkha, Karnal, Bahadurgarh and Raso(Haryana) had started earthworm breeding centres.

TABLE—7.4

Budget estimates for pilot project for wormiculture

Non-Recurring Expenses

Particulars	*Expenses*
Land: 2 Acres with assured irrigation and power facility	Free Lease
Installation of sprinkling system for irrigation of 24 wormicompost sheds. (2 for multiplication of earthworms) with 1 HP electric motor, PVC pipes of 5 and 2.5 cms diameter with 480 nozzle sufficient length of PVC pipes, Storage tank	1,50,000
Construction of 24 sheds each of 100 ft. long 7.5 ft. wide and 6 ft. height for 75 sq. ft. plinth with PVC lining at Rs.2,500/- per shed.	2,20,000
Power - driven chall - cutter with electric motor and belt pulley	25,000
20 wheel - barrows 10 spades, 50 Iron Baskets. 20 rakes, 10 Buckets, 50 Bamboo baskets etc.	15,000
Compost packing yard 1500 sq. ft. with asbestos roof	20,000
Weighing Machine	10,000
One Motor Cycle	20,000
Publicity, Telephone, Stationery and other expenses	10,000

Recuring Expenses

Particulars	*Expenses*
One Manager/and one salesman clerk at Rs.5,000 P.M.	60,000
12 men for sieving garbage 10 trucks a day @ Rs.2,000 P.M. (2000x12x12 persons)	2,88,000
4 workmen for segregation of garbage	36,000

and transferring sheds	
Electricity and water charges	15,000
Rs. 1250 P.M.	
Wormicastings	5,000
Cost of empty bags of 25 Kgs each	
@ Rs.5 / 1670 MTS X 40 bags per MT x Rs.5/per bag	3,34,000
Miscellaneous supervision charges	30,000
5000 trucks of bio-degradable compost	1250 MT
(5000 x 2.5 MT)	Free
1200 trucks of cow manure (1200x3.5 MT)	4200 MT
	6,00,000
Total weight of wormi - compost recovered	16700 MT
at 10 % of the total product.	
Yield of compst at 10 % of total weight	1670 MT
Total Expenditure	13,68,000
Anticipated Receipt:	
Wormicompost recovery.	
(1670 MTs x Rs.2000 per MT)	33,40,000
Net profit in two years	19,72,000

Source : Dr. L. Venkataratnam, Kisan World, May 1994.

IIT DELHI — PROF. MIRA MADAN'S GROUP

Extensive research work has been carried out in the field of vermicomposting, the latest biotechnology where in earthworms are used in composting waste-biomass. Two species of earthworms *Meta phire posthuma, Amynthas morrisi,* collected from the northern region of India, were found to be quite efficient in converting the waste biomass (Kitchen waste, vegetable waste and other agricultural waste) into vermicompost. The methodology for earthworm culturing and compost making was standardized.

The vermicompost was tried on two crops—maize and wheat in pots as well as at the field level. These crops were grown on different agrowaste like garbage, compost, slurry, sewage sludge, poultry waste, saw dust waste etc. The research shows that there was significant increase in uptake of macronutrients (N,P,K) in both the crops when earthwroms were applied along with waste. The vermicompost was also tried on a pulse crop (moong). Some lignolytic, cellulolytic and pectinolytic fungi were isolated from the various herbivorous dungs.

KERALA AGRICULTURAL UNIVERSITY

A group of scientists involving Prof P.Padmja, Dr P. Prabhakumari, Smt T.Jiji, and Dr Ushakumari have evaluated the efficacy of different epigeic earthworm species and have selected the most efficient ones based on their breeding and compost production potential. Simple vermicomposting technologies were standardised for composting farm and vegetable market waste as well as kitchen waste.

Experiments are in progress to standardise the dose of vermi compost as a source of organic manure for tropical vegetable crops and as a partial or full substitute of inorganic fertilizers. Experiments are also in progress to study the effect of vermicomposting/ vermiculture in situ on physical and chemical properties of soil and pest and disease incidence on vegetable crops.

Future plans of the groups include studies on:

i) efficiency of vermicompost/vermiculture in situ for the major crops of Kerala

ii) possibility of substitution of inorganic fertilizers by vermicompost/vermiculture for major crops

iii) tolerance of earthworms for different pesticides and fungicides applied to crops

iv) survey of local earthworm and selection of the most efficient species for compost production

v) efficiency of vermiculture for amelioration of problem soils and also for pollution control

MARATHAWADA AGRICULTURAL UNIVERSITY, COLLEGE OF AGRICULTURE, PARBHANI

Dr R.S. Raut and Dr O.D. Kohire have been involved in the follow ing studies:

i) the screening of earthworms for utilization of agricultural waste for production of vermicompost

ii) the production of Vermicompost for commercial use in agriculture

iii) assessing the relative performance of vermicompost for improvement of degrated soils for sustainable agriculture

iv) production of cocoons for commercial utilization

v) development of technology for mass production of vermiculture and vermicompost.

The group has published the following papers/reports:

i) R.S. Raut, S.S. Mane and Kohire O.D. (1993)

Use of earthworms for improvement of alkali soils for sustainable agriculture. Paper presented at congress on traditional science and technologies of India held at IIT, Powai Bombay from 28 Nov-3 Dec. 1993.

ii) R.S. Raut, S.S. Mane and Kohire O.D. (1994)

Relative performance of vermicompost use in improvement of alkali soil for sustainable agriculture. Report presented at AGRESCO SUB-COMMITTEE, held at Marathwada Agricultural University, Parbhani on 28th April, 1994.

iii) Kohire O.D. and R.S. Raut (1994). Gandul Katache wadhate Mahatwa, Marathi Bulletin pp - 19-24.

8

R&D ON VERMITECHNOLOGY AT THE CENTRE FOR POLLUTION CONTROL AND ENERGY TECHNOLOGY

S. Gajalakshmi @ Suja*

WATER HYACINTH AS A SUBSTRATE FOR VERMICOMPOSTING

Of the overall biomass growing in the world, as much as 33% comes from aquatic vegetation. How much of this is contributed by aquatic weeds like water hyacinth *(Eichhornia crassipes* Mart Solms), salvinia *(Salvinia molesta,* Mitchell), hydrilla *(Hydrilla verticillata)* and others, has not yet been estimated; but the contribution is likely to be immense considering the fact that some of these species produce more biomass per unit area than even the most prolific of their terrestrial counterparts (Abbasi 1987)

The ease of reproduction through vegetative propagation, high tolerance towards environmental fluctuations, capability to grow on bad quality as well as good quality waters—all these factors combine to make aquatic weeds like water hyacinth and salvina as forceful colonisers of water bodies (Gupta 1979). In fact, many authors

* Ms. S. Gajalakshmi @ Suja MSc, M.Phil, is a Junior Scientist with Centre for Pollution Control and Energy Technology

consider the growth potential of water hyacinth and salvinia are the ultimate achievable by any plant, terrestrial or aquatic, on earth (Abbasi & Nipaney 1986). These attributes of aquatic macrophytes—such as water hyacinth and salvinia—promotes them as suitable bioagents in aquatic macrophyte based wastewater treatment systems—AMS (Abbasi 1995, Abbasi and Nipaney 1993, 1994; Abbasi and Ramasamy 1999). However when these macrophytes occupy lakes, ponds and the proliferation of the same in an uncontrolled manner leads to the deterioration of water quality of the water bodies and becomes a major threat to the environment (Abbasi 1987).

Weed menace : The aquatic weeds cause immense harm to water resources by occupying lakes, ponds and canals and thus reducing the carrying capacity of these water bodies. The evapotranspiration by the weeds causes water loss several times higher than the loss due to evaporation from weed - free surfaces. They interfere with fisheries and inland navigation. They also harm the water quality in several ways : cutting off sunlight from reaching the water; reducing the dissolved oxygen levels of the water; polluting water through decay; causing stagnation and thereby supporting growth of mosquitoes and flies; impeding the growth of useful aquatic organisms such as fishes and prawns, & so on. The combined impact of all these factors can be strong enough to cause tremendous hardships to people and jeopardise the entire economy of the affected region. Attempts to destroy the weeds with chemicals or bioagents (insects, snails, ducks, fishes, rat etc) have failed throughout the world. At best such attempts only bring temporary relief because some or the other weed soon replaces the destroyed one. Worst still, introduction of bioagents or chemicals on a large scale carries the grave risk of ecological damage (Abbasi 1987).From the survey of the past efforts it is noticed that the heavy initial clearance of the weed from the water bodies followed by regular periodic removal of the regrown weeds and proper utilization of the harvested weeds seem to be a viable solution to the weed menace. Among the various available options the one which holds great promise and is compatible with the weeds high growth potential is convertion to energy via anaerobic digestion. Among the various anaerobic digestion technologies, multi-phase fermentation and high-solids digestion are the most suitable techniques available for the utilization of aquatic weeds to generate energy (Abbasi et al 1992a, 1992b; Abbasi and Ramasamy 1996, 1999; Ramasamy and Abbasi 2000). However, all such weed-utilization processes ultimately lead to the following problems:

a) high volume of sludges (spent weed) are generated at the end of the process. These solid biowastes generally associated with malodour poses serve threat to the environment and public health if they are not properly disposed.

b) possibility of infestation of the weeds from the sludges (spent weed)due to the presence of viable seeds or vegetative propagules. (Abbasi and Ramasamy, 1996)

Our present R&D efforts are focussed to meet this challenge by vermicomposting water hyacinth as such and weed-based sludge (spent weed resulting from the multi-phase fermentors and high-solids digesters).

Response of earthworms to water hyacinth as feed

It is well-known that animals don't prefer water hyacinth as a source of food. This is true of rumens, fish, down to invertebrates (Abbasi et al 1988). One of the reasons is that the weed is low in nutrients. Presence of disagreeble chemicals is lilkely to be another major factor.

When earthworms were put on beds prepared with water hyacinth, they tended to migrate for search of better food. When their exit routes were closed, they seemed to reluctantly feed on water hyacinth. There was significant earthworm mortality, and those who survived evidenced loss of weight and slow reproduction.To circumvent this problem we have conducted extensive experiments on developing strategies to acclimatise earthworms with water hyacinth. The following practice is found to be effective.

a) Initially water hyacinth with which the worms are to be acclimatized has to be mixed with cow dung in the required ratio and this feed has to be fed to the vermireactors for atleast two weeks.

b) The proportion of the cowdung in the feed mixture has to be reduced in a systematic manner and finally it has to be eliminated completely. (This process may take another few weeks depending upon the feed material.)

c) Now this water hyacinth has to be continued as feed for atleast one month. The percent conversion and changes in worm biomass are to be monitored systematically during the period of acclimatization.

Thus the worms have now been acclimatized to water hyacinth.

Effect of acclimatization on the conversion efficiency of water hyacinth into vermicastings

The following experiments (Figure 8.1) were conducted to study the effect of acclimatization on the conversion efficiency of the weed into vermicasts. The feed material water hyacinth was mixed with cowdung in the ratio of 6:1 (six parts of water hyacinth and one part of cow dung) was subjected to acclimatized and non-acclimatized worms. The experiments were done in tetraplicates. Eight vermireactors were fed with a feed consisting water hyacinth mixed with cowdung, out of which four vermireactors were inoculated with acclimatized worms and the other four with non-acclimatized worms. Similarly another set of eight vermireactors were fed with a feed consisting only water hyacinth (not mixed with cowdung) out of these four vermireactors were inoculated with acclimatized worms and other four vermireactors were with non-acclimatized worms. Initially, each of the vermireactors were inoculated with known biomass of worms. Known and equal amount of the feeds were fed to the respective vermireactors—Casts were harvested after 15 days. The increase in number and biomass of the worms were recorded.

The addition of cow dung to the water hyacinth feed in the ratio 6:1 has a major influence on the recovery of castings while the worms used in the vermireactor are of non-acclimatized category. In the case of vermireactors with acclimatized worms, the difference in percent conversion is quite less between the cowdung mixed and non-mixed water hyacinth feeds.

Thus, by the process of acclimatization the efficiency of the worms in converting the water hyacinth (without addition of cowdung) into vermicastings can be increased significantly. Also, the worms get so much accustomed to the water hyacinth feed that

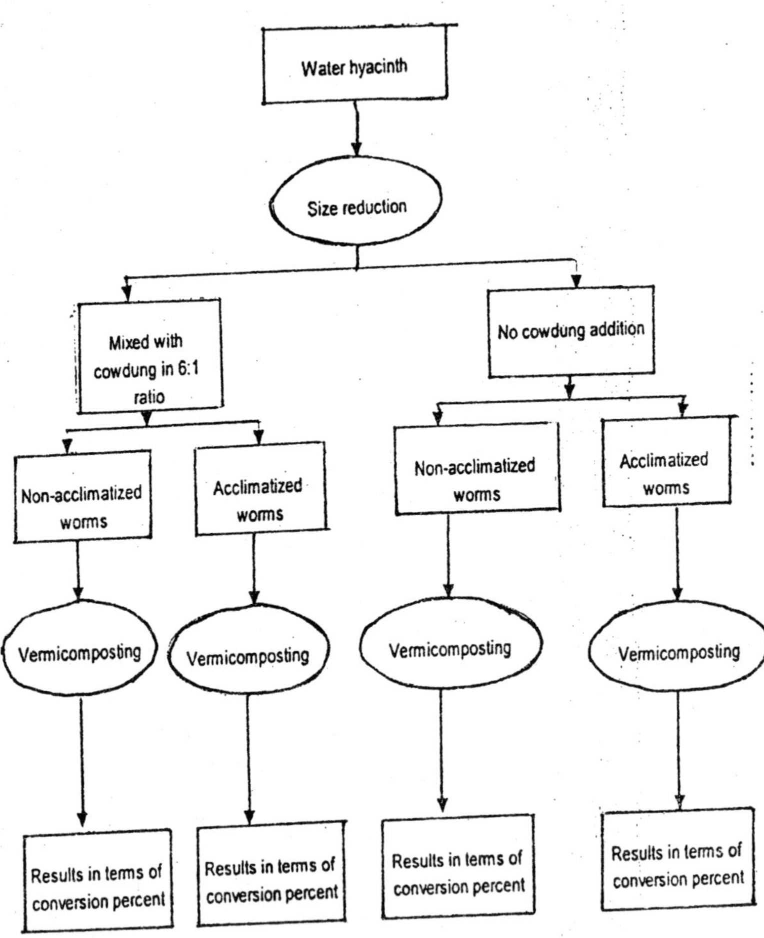

Figure 8.1
Flowsheet indicating the design of the experiments to study the impact of acclimatization of the worms

even the addition of cowdung can be eliminated and only water hyacinth can be fed as feed without affecting the recovery of vermicastings.

Studies on the impact of precomposting on the conversion efficiency of water hyacinth into vermicastings

Certain wastes containing organic matter (eg vegetable matter, paper, cardboard, meat, food wastes etc) when subjected directly to vermireactors are not accepted by the worms. Of the several reasons mentioned for such failure the major ones are that the worms could not withstand the heat generated by fresh urban wastes and presence of certain undesirable organisms like insects and weeds (Bhiday 1995, Abbasi and Ramasamy 1999). Hence a pre - treatment stage becomes inevitable when such wastes are to be treated using vermicomposting technology. Similar observation is also made by many others, to cite a few : according to Edwards (1995), unlike traditional composting in which the temperature might rise about 70°C at certain point of time, vermicomposting systems must be maintained at temperature below 35°C. Exposure of earthworms to temperatures above this, even for short periods, will kill them. Seenappa and Jaganatha Row (1995) have observed that, the adaptability of earthworms to different types of organic wastes could be achieved and to make such waste more palatable the waste has to be aerated in rotor drums in order to encourage aerobic microbes before feeding the waste to earthworms. Thus the common solution to increase the palatability of the waste and to avoid the danger of heat and other pests is a pre-treatment or preprocessing or pre-composting (Bhiday 1995, Edwards 1995, Abbasi and Ramasamy 1996; 1999)

The following experiments were conducted to study the impact of precomposting/pretreatment on the conversion efficiency of water hyacinth into vermicastings. The design of the experiments is given in the form of a flow-sheet (Figure 8.2). The experiments were done in tetraplicates.

(1) A set of four vermi-reactors were fed with water hyacinth mixed with cowdung in 6:1 ratio (non - precomposted).

(2) Another set of four vermireactors were fed with precomposted weed mixture. The precomposted weed mixture was prepared by the following method : chopped

water hyacinth partially decomposed along with garden soil and cowdung in the ratio of 6:3:1 (water hyacinth: soil: cowdung) The mixture was allowed to decompose aerobically in a wide-mouthed earthern vessel for 7 days. It was moistured periodically and also covered loosely with a wet cloth in order to prevent the loss of moisture through evaporation and thereby to facilitate the decomposition.

(3) A set of four vermireactors were fed with water hyacinth alone (not mixed with cowdung and non-precomposted).

Known and equal quantities of feeds were fed to the respective vermireactors. Initially each vermireactor was inoculated with known biomass of worms. Casts were harvested after every 25 days. The increase in number of biomass of worms were recorded.

Water hyacinth when subjected to aerobic precomposting for 7 days becomes partly decomposed by the activity of soil microbes. Such partly decomposed water hyacinth is more palatable to the worms. When the water hyacinth is applied as such fresh the recovery of castings is less and the heat generated during the initial period might have affected the worm population also, which in turn affects adversely the recovery of vermicasts. Thus the precomposting step is essential for water hyacinth when subjected to vermicomposting as it enhances the rate of conversion considerably.

Studies on the spent weed disposal through vermicomposting

As mentioned earlier, of the several options available on the utilization of aquatic weeds (NAS 1976, Abbasi and Nipaney 1984, 1986) the one which holds promise on a large scale, compatible with their high growth potential is conversion to energy through anaerobic fermentation (Abbasi 1987, Abbasi and Ramasamy 1996, 1999).

We have tried to meet this challenge by vermicomposting weed-based sludge (spent weed resulting from the acid-phase fermentation of *E.crassipes)* and apply the compost to the soil.

The following experiments were conducted to study the disposal of spent weed through vermicomposting. The experiments were done in tetraplicates. Four vermireactors were fed with spent

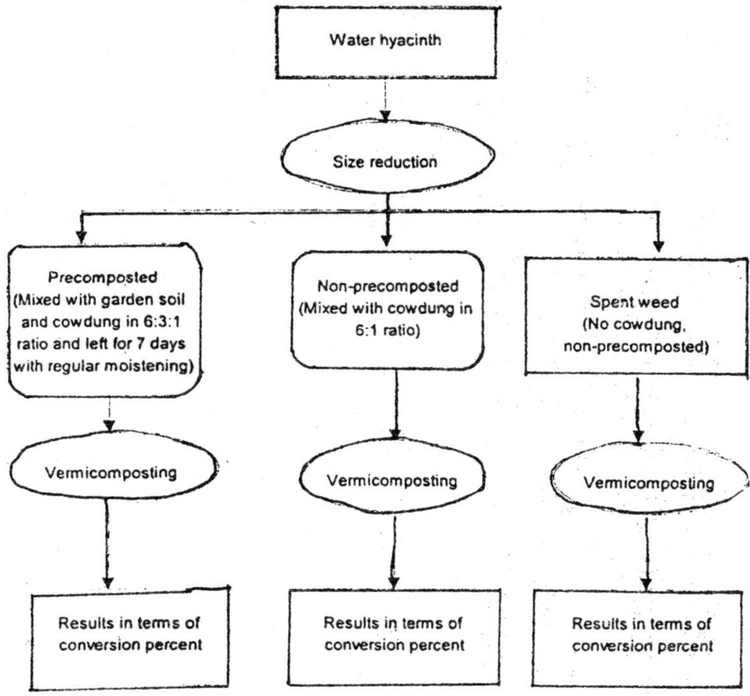

Figure 8.2
Flowsheet indicating the design of the experiments to study the impact of precomposting

weed mixed with cow dung; four vermireactors were fed with precomposted spent weed and another four with spent weed only (i.e. with no cowdung and non-precomposted). Known and equal quantities of the feeds were fed to the respective vermireactors. Casts were harvested at 15 days interval. The increase in the number and biomass of the worms were recorded.

Another set of experiments were conducted using acclimatized and non-acclimatized worms to test the effect of acclimatization on the conversion efficiency of the worms. The experiments were done in teraplicates. Eight vermireactors were fed with precomposted spent weed, four with acclimatized worms and another four with non-acclimatized worms.

Among all the forms of water hyacinth used as feed, the spent weed obtained from acid phase fermenters seem to be the best feed as far as the per cent conversion of the feed into vermicasts is concerned. The additional experiment has confirmed our earlier findings that acclimatization improves the conversion percentage considerably in the case of spent weed also.

Thus based on the results in terms of per cent conversion and worm biomass it may be concluded that the spent weed is the best feed among the feeds (water hyacinth) so far tried in this centre. This may be due to the following reasons:

1) The water hyacinth when subjected to acid phase fermentation in which both aerobic and anaerobic microbes are involved—the feed gets partly digested and becomes soft, in other words becomes palatable to the worms;

2) during the process of acid phase fermentation certain amount of cowdung is added as inoculum, thus the feed get appropriate amount of nitrogen.

3) further when such pre-treated or pre-digested spent weed is subjected to precomposting it becomes more palatable to the worms.

PAPER AS A SUBSTRATE FOR VERMICOMPOSTING

Paper is one of the major constituent of solid waste.It is a stable material that biodegrades slowly with low potential toxicity. Disposal of paper is a major problem since it cannot be effectively composted. It is usually disposed of in landfill sites. Paper waste is almost entirely made up of cellulosic material but has negligible concentration of nutrients. Thus it is a tougher challenge to use paper as a substrate for vermicomposting than even aquatic weeds like water hyacinth. In India and elsewhere, particularly in the third world, paper waste produced by households and small-sized offices is disposed in trash bins along with other types of solid and semi-solid wastes. It eventually adds up to the large quantities of municipal solid waste that is typically piled up on land by the side of households, agricultural fields, and highways, posing serious environmental pollution problem.

In larger institutions such as the university where the authors work, paper waste in periodically piled up and set on fire, causing air pollution as also wastage of otherwise utilizable carbon contained in the paper. Only from very large offices, which produce paper waste of the order of a few tons per week, is such waste taken for reuse in kraft paper mills.

The authors have been trying to develop effective yet low-cost technology for utilizing different components of municipal solid waste (MSW); for example solid-feed anaerobic digestion to produce methane (Ramasamy and Abbasi 1999, 2000 a), and extraction of volatile fatty acids from agrowastes followed by methanogenesis, (Abbasi et al 1992, Abbasi and Ramasamy 1999, Ramasamy and Abbasi 2000 b). As a part of these initiatives, vermicomposting of paper waste has been attempted. The several likely advantages of this utilization option are: a) it is capable of handling very low to very high quantities of paper waste, b) it is simple and low-cost, thus appropriate for use at household level in cities/towns, and in villages, c) it can handle 'unclean' paper (for example paper mixed with food waste) thus saving the step of washing the paper prior to vermiconversion, and d) the vermicasts have a very popular and ready market as enrichers of soil.

Choice of earthworm species

Drawida willsi, Eudrilus eugeniae, Lampito mauritii, and *Perionyx excavatus* are classified as epigeics or humus feeder earthworms. They typically inhabit humus-laden upper layers of soil and manure-pits. They have higher frequency of reproduction and faster rate of growth to adulthood—the two factors which make them efficient utilizers of humus, manure, and other forms of organic carbon. Further, as they don't burrow deep into the soil, the vermireactors based on them need not cortain deep bed of soil. This contributes to saving on reactor volume, in turn contributing to favourable economics.

Of the four species used by us, *E. eugeniae* has been the most popular for vermicomposting, of cowdung. *L.mauritii* and *P. excavatus* have been used to a lesser extent. The least studied is *D. willsi*; we have chosen it because it is endemic to Southern India and might prove more hardy and resilient in the agroclimatic conditions of this part of India.

Vermireactors

Circular, 4 litre plastic containers (dia 24 cm, depth 9 cm) were filled from bottom up with successive layers of sawdust river sand and soil of depths 1 cm, 2 cm, and 4 cm respectively. In each reactor, 20 healthy and adult animals of chosen species were introduced. The reactor bed were maintained moisture by periodic sprinkling of adequate quantities of water.

The reactors were fed with pieces of paper (as they occurred in the waste taken from trash bins) soaked in water for 7 days. On the seventh day, it was taken squeezed and then mixed with cowdung in required ratio. All quantities were adjusted so that the feed mass reported in this paper represents dry weights (taken after oven-drying at 105°C to constant weight). The castings were also quantified after oven drying at 105°c to constant weights.

The reactors, all run in duplicates, were started with 75 g of feed comprising of paper waste: cowdung in 4:1 w/w ratio. After 15 days the castings and the earthworms were removed in separate containers for quantification while the rest of the reactor contents were discarded. Within a few minutes fresh reactors were started with everything else the same except a) the 75 g feed now had paper and cowdung in 5:1 w/w ratio, and b) of the earthworms removed from the previous run, the juveniles were separated and the 20 worms, with which the reactors were started, were weighed and reintroduced. It was very easy to distinguish 'parent' worms as they Owere much larger in size to the juveniles produced during the 7-day run. The process was repeated after a week, shifting to the feed still leaner in cowdung-with paper: cowdung: : 6:1 (w/w). This gradual shift to increasingly paper-rich (or cowdung-lean) feed was done so that the earthworms get an opportunity to acclimatise themselves. All subsequent measurements were taken fortnightly, resetting the vermireactors each time so that the same sets of worms with which the reactors were started, continued to be the main producers of vermicasts.

After six months of operation, at which point this report is being submitted, the performance of all the reactors in terms of conversion of feed to vermicasts has improved slowly, yet steadily.

All the 160 animals of four species with which eight reactors were started six months back, continue to gain in wait and produce offspring's. On an average, the individuals of *D.willsi, L.mauritii*, and *P.excavatus* have grown to more than twice their initial weights. The individuals of *E.eugeniae* were heavier at the outset, and have grown in weight by about 34%. But *E.eugeniae* have been most reproductive, followed by the next most no heavy L.mauritii. The two lighter-weight species D.willsi and *P.excavatus* have each produced significantly lesser number of offspring's. It follows that if separate vermireactors are set with the four species studied in this work, the reactors with *E.eugeniae* and *L.mauritii* would not only produce more casts per worm, but would also generate more rapidly increasing worm population thus helping the vermiconversion further.

Role of Pretreatment or Precomposting in Vermicomposting

The worms when fed with paper directly without any pretreatment, suffered loss of weight and some experienced mortality. The paper was soaked in limited quantity of water and then mixed with cow dung in the required ratios. The worms preferred the latter feed. Hence pretreatment or precomposting the feed is essential for better conversion.

Role of texture of the feed

The feed texture does influence the feeding activity apart from the chemical composition in acceptance of feed by worms. As experienced by the authors, the paper as such was not palatable to the worms whereas the paper when soaked becomes softer and palatable to the worms.

9

SOME PROMINENT EXPERTS

We present in this chapter brief write-ups on some of the experts who have made significant contributions vis a vis the pure and the applied aspects of vermitechnology.

The list is by no means exhaustive and we hope to suitably update it in the subsequent editions of this book. The sequence in which the experts have been described follows the alphabetical order of the surnames; no hierarchy is implied in the order.

Dr U.S.Bhawalkar

Dr Bhawalkar is the Director of Bhawalkar Earthworm Research Institute(BERI), Pune. His bio-brief :

Born	:	16-2-1951
Graduation	:	B.Tech (Chemical Engg.) IIT Bombay, April 1973
PhD	:	Ph.D Chemical Engg. with specialisation in Vermiculture Biotechnology, IIT Bombay, 1994.

Dr Bhawalkar started BERI in June 1981 in Pune to develop vermiculture biotechnology for

(i) environmental protection

(ii) sustainable agriculture, and

(iii) wasteland development

Dr. Bhawalkar being a chemical engineer, with 12 years of practical experience with diverse species of earthworms, could develop field-scale applications of vermiculture first time in the world. (Though there are about 4,000 earthworm research papers published to-date, none refer to successful field-scale applications).

He has developed practical cost-effective packages for sustainable agriculture, wasteland development and effective waste management: They include the following :

a) thousands of city people are using BERI's vermiculture package to bioprocess their kitchen residues in their gardens on the ground or in the balcony or on the terrace;

b) he has developed unique packages for management of organic waste; solid and liquid residues from the society and agro-industries are being used as valuable raw materials for bioconversion into vermicastings, the sustainable effective biofertiliser for the soil;

c) his unique contribution to the field of vermiculture is the process of wastewater treatment—this provides a novel method for treating the organic wastewaters to produce vermicastings and water for reuse. He is now in the process of exporting Beri Vermifilter (BV) packages to other countries, both developed and underdeveloped.

Dr Bhawalkar and BERI have received several recognitions :

i) Dr Bhawalkar was honoured by the prestigious Rolex Award for Enterprise Secretariat by his inclusion in their book 'Spirit of Enterprise - '1990'.

ii) BERI received an 'Outstanding Exhibit' award at the National Fair on Water Management in Agriculture, Madras, March 1990. The exhibit was a live demonstration of purification of wastewater BV the by process to get water for irrigation and vermicastings, the effective biofertilizer.

iii) Dr Bhawalkar was honoured by Rotary Club of Pune Central, June 1992 for his contribution to environmental protection of the city of Pune, by motivating individual families—with active support from the Save Pune Citizens Committee—to recycle kitchen and garden residues, with vermiculture biotechnology.

iv) Dr Bhawalkar was appointed as a member of the 'committee on sustainable agriculture', set up by the Government of Maharashtra. The committee strongly recommended the government to popularize effective recycling of agricultural residues by the farmers, to cut down the non-renewable external inputs.

v) BERI was honoured in July 1992 by the Late Shri Sharad Kelkar Memorial Award Committee, instituted by State Industrial and Investment Corporation of Maharashtra (SICOM) with a cash award and a certificate of recognition, for BERI's research related to industrial waste-management with vermiculture biotechnology.

vi) BERI was invited by the Rotary Club of Makati Ayala, Metro Manila, The Philippines, to conduct a seminar on 'Waste Management with Vermiculture Biotechnology', in November 1992.

vii) BERI was awarded a contract to design 'sewage treatment plant through vermiculture for small communities' by the Central Pollution Control Board, New Delhi.

viii) In addition to more than 30 national seminars, Dr Bhawalkar has presented papers in 9 international conferences.

Dr. H.R.Bhiday

Professor Bhiday is the Director of INORA (Institute of Natural Organic Agriculture for Sustainable Development). Dr. Bhiday took his first PhD from Nagpur University (1954) and second PhD from University of London (1959). After a long and very distinguished career as physicists he has established INORA and deeply involved himself with it besides, of course, holding several other senior positions.

Dr. Bhiday is among the first to have developed commercial scale "vermicomposting" units in India. Before starting work on earthworm biotechnology, he made films on earthworm biology and vermicomposting. He also visited different farmers in the United States to know more about the role of earthworms in organic farming. He studied the status of organic farming in India during early 1980s.

The summary of Dr Bhiday's past work pertaining to earthworm biotechnology is given below:

1. made videofilms on wormicomposting and organic farming;
2. used these films for talking to huge gatherings of farmers;
3. produced first PhD in the field of, 'Communication of earthworm technology to farmers';
4. tried earthworm technology on vast acreages in Maharashtra. Most of the results are successful;
5. has travelled extensively across India to talk to farmers and to spread the technology.

Dr. Bhiday's recent activities include :

1. establishment of INORA;
2. working on several projects on waste management by wormicomposting, organic farming and wasteland development;
3. establishment of 22 INORA centres throughout India.

His future plans :

1. educating masses in organic farming, wormicomposting. and water management through tutored video instruction scheme;
2. developing organic farms throughout the country—the 21 INORA centres will act as satellites and proper networking will be developed to get maximum data;
3. establishing an exclusive training centre on organic farming.

Dr A.D.Bhide

Dr Bhide is Scientist and Head, Solid Waste Management Divison at NEERI, Nagpur. He had his graduation and Post-graduation (Zoology) from Nagpur University. He was awarded Ph.D at Nagpur University in the year 1992 for his work on 'Studies on fate of intestinal parasites during refuse composting'.

Since 1969 he is working in NEERI in the area of Solid waste management. His main fields of research in the area of solid waste management are biochemistry of composting, biogas and vermitechnology.

In the area of vermi-technology, he has studied annelidic consumption of organic biomass using *Perionyx excavtus.* Vermicomposting as continuous unit suitable for domestic and institutional purposes has been developed.

Presently, the main field of his research are recycling of municipal solid waste using soild state digestion for biogas and vermicomposting of residue after biomethanation.

Future work is proposed on environmental factors influencing population dynamics of earthworm, studies on microbial decomposition and earthworm consumption of waste and resultant changes in organic biomass. Treatment of sewage employing is proposed. Dr Bhide has authored a paper 'Vermicomposting of vegetable waste', published in Compost Science and Utilization, Autumn 1993, Vol.1 No.2, 1993.

Mr Ravindra Bhole

Mr Bhole is the founder of Bio-Genik Systems, one of the pioneers in vermitechnology. Having completed MSc in organic chemistry from IIT Kharagpur in 1967, he served in various capacities in multinational pharmaceutical companies for over 15 years.

In 1982, he developed interest in vermiculture when he read about it in foreign magazines. He started experimenting with different species of earthworms collected from different locations. There was no information available in Indian Agricultural Universities.

When he read and studied about vermiculture biotechnology, he was convinced that this 'concept' could be propagated in practical manner only if vermiculture breeder boxes are available. So he concentrated his efforts in that direction.

In 1984, he visited wormaries in UK and USA and also met scientists working in the universities. This helped him to get practical hints and selection of proper species useful and efficient for vermicomposting.

Thereafter, he conducted numerous trial experiments to standardise various parameters to make vermiculture breeder boxes. Around 1986, he started making and selling vermiculture breeder boxes. His is the first commercial venture in India. This has helped many to make their own vermicompost.

For concept propagation, he had given talks on TV and giving farmers' meets, seminars and exhibitions. He has also travelled a lot for giving practical guidance on vermicomposting.

In his trials successful vermicomposting is carried out with various wastes like biogas slurry, canteen waste, kitchen waste, food processing industry waste, farm waste, along with cow dung, tea industry waste, etc.

Bio-Genik Systems reputed clients include (besides numerous individuals) :

1. Indian Agricultural Research Institute, New Delhi
2. College of Agriculture, Pune
3. BAIF Research Foundation, Pune
4. SULABH International Institute of Technical Research and Consultancy, Delhi
5. Rashtrapati Bhavan, New Delhi
6. IIT Bombay
7. INORA Trust, Pune
8. Central Pollution Control Board, Delhi
9. Sayan Sugar Works, Surat, Gujarat

10. Konkan Krishi Vidyapeeth, Dapoli
11. Yuvak Vikas Kendra, Bijapur
12. Vasantdada Sugar Institute, Majari, Pune
13. Maharashtra Agricultural Bioteks, Pune
14. RBT Tea Estate, Cochin

Dr Madhab C.Dash

Dr Madhab C.Dash is a senior faculty member in Ecology in School of Life Sciences, Sambalpur University. He obtained the Doctorate degree from Calgary, Canada. He did his B.Sc and M.Sc from the Utkal University. He is working in Sambalpur University from the year 1976.

Dr. Dash has authored seven books/monographs (Academic Press, USA, John Wiley, USA, Elsivier, Netherland, Cambridge University Press, U.K.).

Pioneering and original contributions have been made by Dr. Dash to the understanding of culture techniques, metabolic functions and energetics, community structure and functional role of soil oligochaetes. The studies could show the academic and practical importance of earthworms with regard to secondary production and vermitechnology.

Dr M.C.Dash has published nearly 84 papers, out of which 70 papers are on oligochaeta (Earthworms and Euchytrachids) biology/ ecology and vermitechnology of which 5 papers are on vermicomposting. They are :

1. Dash, M.C. (1978). *The role of earthworms in the decomposer system.* (In Glimpses of Ecology). International Scientific Publication, Jaipur, India, 399-409.
2. Dash, M.C. and Patra, U.C. (1979). *Wormcast production and nitrogen contribution to soil by a tropical earthworm publication from a grassland site in Orissa, India*, Rev. Ecol. Biol. Sol. 16, 79-87.
3. Senapati, B.K., and Dash, M.C. (1982). *Earthworm as waste conditioner* Indian Engg. Jour. X (2), 53-57.

4. Dash, M.C., and Senapati, B.K. (1985). *Vermitechnology : Potentiality of Indian earthworms for vermicomposting and vermifeed.* (In soil Biology, Proc. Nat. Symp. On current Trends in soil biol.) HAU Hissar, India. 61-69.

5. Dash, M.C., and Senapati, B.K. (1986). *Vermitechnology. An option for organic waste management in India. (In Proc. Nat. Sem. Org. Waste Utiliz. Verm. Part B. verms and vermicomposting)*, Orissa, India, 157-172.

Dr Surya Gunjal

Dr Surya Gunjal, M.Sc. (Agri), Microbiology, Ph.D Agro-biotechnology is presently working as a Director of School of Agricultural Sciences at Yashwantrao Chavan Maharashtra Open University, Nasik (MS). He is mainly associated with the task of disseminating advanced and appropriate knowledge in the field of agriculture, horticulture and sericulture including agro-biotechnology, among the farmers through Krishi Prayog Pariwar system.

Dr Gunjal has undertook research trials on utilising vermiculture in grape production in Nasik district of Maharashtra. He has succeeded in replacing chemical fertilizers in grape production practices in some parts of Nasik area. He has planned to try out organic farming mainly with the help of vermiculture in the fruit gardens including grape, pomegranate, mango, custard apple etc.

Dr Gunjal's publications include :

1. *Organic farming : A need for rethinking*
   A marathi article in Gavakari news paper Nasik, 1991.

2. *Principles of organic farming*
   A paper presented in national seminar on organic farming at Pune, 1992.

3. *Grape cultivation through earthworm farming*
   A paper presented in national seminar on organic farming at Pune, 1992.

4. *Mycorrhizal control of wilt in Casuarina*
   A paper published in Agroforestry today, ICRAF, Nairobi, Kenya.

5. *Soil microflora and plant growth*
   A paper presented in the national seminar on grape production at Pune, 1991.

6. *Bioorganic manure from sugarcane trash*
   An article published in Marathi, Nasik, 1991.

Dr Sultan Ahmed Ismail

Dr Sultan Ahmed Ismail is the Director, Institute of Research in Soil Biology and Biotechnology (IRSBB), The New College, Madras. He has earned his B.Sc, M.Sc., M.Phil and Ph.D degrees from Madras University. He also holds a Diploma in Higher Education.

Dr. Ismail feels that only endemic species should be used for vermicomposting for a number of reasons including the fact that the bio-energetics of local earthworms are much more favourable for tropical conditions. Dr Ismail has co-authored two books 'Aspects of Behaviour' and 'Composting through earthworm', 1993.

Dr Ismail's article featured in numerous newspapers on a number of occasions.

He has published 39 research papers, out of which 25 papers are on earthworms, of which 1 paper is on vermicomposting :

Ismail, S.A., et al. (1993). 'Composting through earthworms', The New College Madras, 38 pp.

Dr R.D.Kale

Dr R.D.Kale is senior faculty of the Agricultural University, Bangalore. Work on vermiculture was started in the university in 1974. The studies have been mainly related to the ecological aspects of vermiculture and on application of vermiculture technology to agricultural systems.

She has authored about 51 papers out of which 47 papers are on earthworms and of which 7 papers are on vermicomposting. They are :

1. Kale, R.D., and Kubra Bano. (1986). *Field trials with vermicompost* an organic fertilizer. Ibid. pp 151-157.

2. Kubra Bano and Kale, R.D. (1987). *Vermicomposting—A rural technology.* Agricultural Technology 5: 33-34.

3. Kale, R.D. *Role of earthworms in biodegradation of organic wastes.*

4. Kale, R.D. (1992). *Influence of vermicompost application on the available macronutrients and selected microbial populations in a paddy field.* Soil. Biol. Biochem. 24 : 1317-1320.

5. Kale, R.D., and Sunitha, N.S. (1992). *Utilization of earthworms in recycling of household refuse.* (In press). Proceedings of the workshop on Biogas slurry utilization, October 92 CORT.

6. Kale, R.D. (1993). *Vermiculture—A low cost technology for Indian farmers* (in press). Proc. Seminar on Bio-Technology. (Feb, 15 and 16, 1993). State Bank Institute of Rural Development, India.

7. Senapathi, B.K., Kale, R.D., and Dash, M.C. *Vermicomposting : The present state of art.*

Prof Mira Madan

Dr Mira Madan recently retired as Professor from IIT Delhi. Dr Madan has been associated with Centre for Rural Technology at IIT Delhi and has pioneered such biotechnological R&D as use of weeds for mushroom culture and vermicomposting. The publications of Dr Madan include :

1. Madan, M. and Sharma, N. 1984. *Earthworms can fetch fortune.* Farmer's Journal 3 (No.5) : 19-20.

2. Madan, M. and Sharma, N. 1984. *Waste Recycling and utilization through earthworms.* In International Conference on earthworms and waste, Cambridge 23-27, July, p. 26.

3. Sharma, V.K., Madan, M. and Sharma, N. 1986. *Biogas Technology in India : The State of Art, Invention Intelligence*, July, Vol.21 (No.7) : 235-240.

4. Madan, M. and Sharma, N. 1986. *Vermicomposting—A Latest Biotechnology, Rural Technology* Journal Vol. 2(No.9) : 21- 28.

5. Sharma, N., Madan, M., Vimal, R.K. and Bhutani, M.M. 1986. *Waste Utilization and Earthworms.* Published in Proceedings Bio-Energy Society Third Convention and Symposium 86, held during 30 Nov. - 2 Dec. at Pune, pp. 318-323.

6. Sharma, N., Madan, M., Vimal., O.P. and Bhutani, M.M. 1986. *Vermicomposting—Effect on Crop Growth.* Published in Proceedings Bio-Energy Society Third Convention and Symposium 86, held during 30 Nov. - 2 Dec. at Pune, pp. 324-329.

7. Madan, M. and Sharma, N. 1986. *'Recycling of Organic Waste through Vermicomposting',* Bioenergy Newsletter 2, 30-31.

8. Sharma, N. and Madan, M. 1987. *Recycling of organic wastes through earthworms for crop growth.* Solar Energy and Rural Development Proceedings of the National Seminar on Solar Energy and Rural Development, Kolhapur (India) May 29-31, pp. 109-119.

9. Sharma, N., Madan, M. and Vimal, O.P. 1987. *Nutrient value of fertilizer obtained by bioconversion of organic wastes for maize crop.* Proceedings Bio-Energy Society, Fourth Convention and Symposium 87, held on 4-5 Sept. at Udaipur, pp. 167-172.

10. Sharma, N., Madan, M. and Sharma, V.K. 1987. *Vermicomposting : Conversion of Waste Biomass into Fertilizer.* Invention Intelligence. Vol. 22 (No.2) 55-59.

11. Sharma, N. and Madan, M. 1987. *An Alternative Method of Insect Pest Control.* Rural Technology Journal, Special issue on Agriculture Vol. 4 (No.3) : 3-4.

12. Sharma, N. and Madan, M. 1987. *Some Methods to determine earthworms pollution in soil* : Indian Journal of Environment and Agriculture, Vol. 2, 129-132.

13. Sharma, N. and Madan, M. 1988. *Earthworms—An alternative source on high quality protein.* Invention Intelligence Vol.23, 164-169.

14. Madan, M. 1988. *Vermicompost. Directory of Rural Technologies.* Published by Council for Advancement of

People's Action and Rural Technology (CAPART), Guru Nanak Foundation Building, New Mehruali Road, New Delhi-67 Vol.2, p. 8.

15. Madan, M., Philip, S., Sharma, N. and Verma, S. 1988. *Utilization of rural wastes through improved bio-technology using earthworms.* Rural Technology Journal. Vol. 4 (No.4) : 7-9.

16. Sharma, N. and Madan, M. 1988. *Effects of various organic wastes alone and with earthworms on the total dry matter yield of wheat and maize.* Biological Wastes 24, 1-8.

17. Sharma, V.K., Sharma, N. and Madan, M. 1989. *Organic Recycling with Earthworms Potential Source for Energy Conservation in India* (Chapter) Energy Resources and Technology—Dr. N.D.Kaushik and Dr S. Kaneff and Sponsorer by Geo-Eviron Academia Jodhpur, pp. 131-175 (Chapter).

18. Sharma, N. and Madan, M. 1993. *Earthworms—Sons of the Soil.* Invention Intelligence. (In Press).

Dr S.P.Patil

Dr Patil is Professor of Entomology at College of Agriculture, Dapoli. He holds B.Sc. (Agri) with Honours, M.Sc. (Agri) and Ph.D degrees. He has undergone advanced training in biological control at England and West Indies.

Dr Patil has carried out preliminary work on

i) survey of earthworm species in the Konkan region

ii) biology of two earthworm species of this region

iii) mass multiplication of *E.foetida and D.affinis*

iv) guided a Post-graduate scholar who worked on species distribution and C:N ratio.

Publications

1. *Preliminary observations on earthworm multiplication.* AU Journal 16.

2. Presented a paper on *'Use of earthworms in agriculture'* during a group discussion on earthworm uses held at Konkan Krishi Vidyapeeth, Dapoli on 3rd September, 1993.

Dr B.K.Senapati

Dr B.K.Senapati, a senior faculty member of School of Life Sciences, Sambalpur University, Orissa, holds a master's degree in Biological Sciences from Sambalpur University in 1980 for his work on 'Aspects of Ecophysiological studies on tropical earthworms'. He is in the area of earthworm ecology and ecotechnology since 1975.

Dr Senapati worked mainly on local species which could take care to biodiversity and system stability. He worked on 20 different Indian species of earthworms. He feels that for vermiculture, any earthworm species can be used, while for vermicomposting, only epigeic or endogeic earthworms can be used.

Dr Senapati has authored 60 publications out of which 52 are on earthworms and of which 10 are on vermitechnology/ vermicomposting. They are :

1. Senapati, B.K., and Dash, M.C. 1984. *Functional role of earthworms in the decomposer sub-system.* Trop. Ecol. (Intl. Soc. Trop. Ecol. India) 25 (2) : 54-73 (Review article).

2. Dash, M.C., and Senapati, B.K. 1985. *Vermitechnology potentiality of Indian earthworms for vermicomposting and vermifeed* Soil Biology, HAU, Hissar, pp 61-70 (Review Article).

3. Dash, M.C., and Senapati, B.K. 1986. *Vermitechnology an option for organic waste management in India. In verms and vermicomposting,* pp 151-172. (Review Article).

4. Senapati, B.K. 1992. *Vermicomposting : An option for recycling of cellulosic wastes of India.* In : New Trends in Biotechnology, New Delhi 347-358.

5. Senapati, B.K. 1993. *Vermitechnology in India. In : Earthowrm resources and vermiculture, Zoological Survey of India* Publ. Zool. Survey (in press).

6. Senapati, B.K., and Dash, M.C. 1982. *Earthworm as waste conditioners*, Industrial Eng. J. (Energy Management issue) XI (2) : 53-57.

7. Senapati, B.K. 1993. *Vermitechnology in India.* In Earthworms resources and vermiculture, pub : Zoological Survey of India (in press).

8. Senapati, B.K. 1993. *Selection of suitable earthworm species for vermicomposting under Indian condition* In : *Earthworm Resources and vermiculture* Pub.Zoological Survey of India (in press).

9. Senapati, B.K. 1993. *Vermitechnology in integrated waste biomass management : concepts, prospects and problems.* In : Biogas slurry utilization, New Delhi 57-74.

10. Senapati, B.K., Lavella, P., and Panigrahi, P.K. 1993. *Vermiculture in plantation crop : and experiment in tea., sustainable farming and the environment* by UPASI (in press).

REFERENCES

Abbasi, S.A. and Nipaney, P.C (1984)

Generation of biogas from Salvinia molesta (Mitchell) on commerical biogas digester. Environmental Technology Letters, 5, 75-80

Abbasi, S.A. and Nipaney, P.C (1986)

Infestation of the fern genus Salvinia: Its status and control. Environmental Conservation, 13, 235-241

Abbasi, S.A. (1987)

Renewable energy from aquatic biomass, In : Proceedings of the 1986 International congress on Renewable Energy sources, CSIC, Madrid, 60

Abbasi, S.A., Nipaney; P.C and Soni, R. (1988)

Aquatic Weeds—Distribution, Impact and Control. Journal of Scientific and Industrial Research 47 650-661

Abbasi, S.A. (1989)

The Most important animal on earth. Mirror 25-26

Abbasi, S.A; Nipaney; P.C and Ramasamy E.V. (1992a)

Use of aquatic weed Salvinia (Salvinia molesta, Mitchell) as full/partial feed in commercial biogas digesters, Indian Journal of Technology, 30, 451-457

Abbasi, S.A; Nipaney; P.C and Ramasamy E.V. (1992b)

Studies on multi-phase anaerobic digestion of Salvinia, Indian Journal of Technology, 30, 483-490

Abbasi, S.A. (1995)

Wastewater treatment with aquatic plants—state-of-the-art report, Scientific contribution number INCOH/SAR-10/95, INCOH secretariat, National Institute of Hydrology, Roorkee India, 50 pages

Abbasi, S.A and Ramasamy E.V. (1996)

Utilization of biowaste solids by extracting volatile fatty acids with subsequent conversion to methane and manure, In : Proceedings of the Twelfth International Conference on Solid Waste Technology and Management, Philadelphia, USA, 401-408.

Abbasi, S.A., and Nipaney; P.C (1993)

World's Worst Weed (Salvinia)—Its Impact and Utilization. International Book Distributers, Dehradun, 226.

Abbasi, S.A., and Nipaney; P.C (1994)

Potential of aquatic weed Salvinia molesta (Mitchell) for water treatment and energy recovery, Indian Journal of Chemical Technology, 1, 204-213

Abbasi, S.A. (1998)

Environmental pollution and its control, Cogent International, Pondicherry, 442 pages

Abbasi, S.A., and Ramasamy E.V.(1999).

Biotechnological Pollution Control Systems; the technologies most appropriate for the third world countries Universities Press of India Ltd., Hyderabad India.

Acharya, C.N, (1939).

Studies on the hot fermentation process for the composting of town refuse and other waste materials II. Some factors influencing the efficacy of the Process Indian Journal of Agricultural Sciences 10, 817 - 833.

Acharya, C.N (1940).

The hot fermentation process for composting of town refuse and other waste materials III the hot fermentation Vs aerobic system of composting. Indian journal of Agricultural Sciences 10, 473 - 488.

Alawdeen, S.S. and Ismail, S.A. (1986).

Stages of growth as a factor in harvesting the earthworm. Lampito mauritii kinberg. Proceedings of National Seminar on Organic Waste Utilization, Vermicomposting Part B. Verms & Vermicomposting. M.C. Dash) B.K. Senapati and P.C. Mishra (Eds) 122-127.

Anstett, A. (1951).

On the macrobiological activation of humification processes, C.R.Agric. Fr., 37, 262-264.

Archangelskii, M.P. (1929).

On the influence of the activity of earthworms on the yield of oats and barley in relation to fertilizer addition, J.landw, Wissensch. Moskau, 6, 849-862.

Arunachalam, S. and Palanichami, S. (1984).

Earthworms as feed for the catfish Mystus vittatus, National Seminar on Organic Waste Utilisation and Vermicomposting.

Ashok Kumar, C. (1994).

State of the Art Report on Vermiculture in India. Council for Advancement of Peoples Action and Rural Technology, New Delhi, 60 pages.

Bano.K, and Kale R.D. (1992).

Potentials of earthworm farming. In: Proceeding of the National Seminar on organic farming Pune, India Mahatma Phulakrishi Vidyapeeth. 45 - 46

Barley, K.P. (1959)

The influence of earthworms on soil fertility II. Consumption of soil and organic matter by the earthworm Allolbophora caliginosa Aust T. agr. Res 10(2) 179-158.

Barley K.P. (1961)

The abundance of earthworms in agricultural land and their possible significance in agriculture. Adv. Agrom.13, 249-68.

Barois, I. and Lavelle, P. (1986).

Changes in respiration rate and some physiochemical properties of a tropical soil during transit through Pontoscolex corethrurus, Soil Biol. Biochem., 539-541.

Bhardwaraj KKR, (1983).

Process—promoting cultures for composting Indian farming 33 5 : 17-19.

Bhawalkar, (1993)

Turning garbage into gold. An Introduction to Vermiculture Biotechnology. Bhawalkar Earthworm Research Institute, Pune.

Bhiday M.R. (1995).

Vermiculturing In : Wealth from Waste S. Khanna and K. Mohan. (Eds) Tata Energy Research Institute New Delhi 138-149.

Bhole, R.J. (1992).

Natural Farming and Vermiculture Biotechnology. Proceedings of National Seminar on Natural Farming L.L. Somani; K.L. Totawat and B.L. Baser (Eds) 143-150.

Blank, E. and Giesecke, F. (1924).

The effect of earthworms on the physical and biological properties of soil, Z.Pflanz. Dung, 3, 198-210.

Bouche, M.B. (1977)

Strategies lombriciennes. In: Soil organisms as components of Ecosystems (eds. U. Lokm and T.persson), Proceedings 6th Int. Soil Lool. Cell.,Ecol. Bull. (stockholm), 25, 122-132.

Bray J.R. and Gorham, E. (1964).

Litter production in forests of the world. Adv.Ecol. Res 2, 101-57.

Bretscher, K. (1896).

The oligochacta of Zurich. Rev. Suisse Zool. 3, 499-532

Byzova, Yu. B.(1965).

Comparative rate of respiration in some earthworms. Rev. Ecol. Biol. Soil. 2, 207-16.

Cohen, S. and Lewis, H.B. (1949).

Nitrogen metabolism of the earthworm Fed. Proc. 8, 191.

Cook, (1983).

The effects of fungi on food selection by Lumbricus terrestris In: Satchell JE (Ed) Earthworm ecology: From Darwin to vermiculture, Chapman and Hall, London, 365-373.

Connet; E and Connett, P. (1994).

Principal Waste Incineration: Wrong Question, wrong Answer. The Ecologist 24.(1)

Darwin, C. (1881)

The formation of vegetable mould through the action of worms, with observations of their habits. Murray, London 326 pp.

Das, A.K. and Dash, M.C. (1989)

Earthworm meal as a protein concentrate for Japanese quails. Indian Journal of Poultry Sciences 24(2). 137-138.

Dash, M.C., Senapathi, B.K., Hota, A.K. and Guru, B.C. (1977).

Observations on the changes in protein, nitrogen, nucleic acid and lipid contents during the development stage of Lampito mauritii, Comp. Physical, Ecol. 2(4): 176-179.

Dash, M.C. (1978).

Role of earthworms in the decomposer system. Off print from Glimpses of Ecology (Prof. R. Misra Commemoration Vol.) Publs. Int. Scientific Publn. 309-406.

Dash, M.C. and Senapathi, B.K. (1985).

Potentiality of Indian earthworms for vermicomposting and vermi feed, In : Proceedings in Soil Biology Symposium Hissar, 61-69.

Dash, M.C. and Senapathi B.K. (1986a).

Vermitechnology, An option for organic waste management in India. Proceedings of National Seminar on Organic Waste Utilization and Vermicomposting Part B: Verms and Vermicomposting, M.C. Dash, B.K. Senapathi and P.C. Mishra (Eds.) 157-172.

Dash, M.C. and Senapathi, B.K. (1986b).

The Earthworm Resource 4: 6-8.

Deeksen, J. (1950).

An electrical method of sampling soil for earthworms. Trans. 4th Int. congr. Soil Sci. 129-31

Dotterweich, H. (1933).

The function of storage of calcium by animals as a buffer reserve in the regulation of reaction. The calciferous glands of earthworms, Pflug. Arch. ges. Physiol. 232, 263-286.

Dusserre, C. (1902).

On the effect of earthworms on the chemical condition of soils, Landw. Jb. Schweiz, 16, 75-78

Eaton, T.H. and Chandler, R.R. (1942).

The fauna of forest humus layers in New Yark. Mem. 247, Cornell Agr. Exp. Stn 26 pp.

Edwards, C.A., (1995)

Historical overview of vermicomposting Biocycle. Journal of composting of recycling 56-58.

Edwards, C.A and Heath; G.W. (1963)

The role of soil animals in breakdown of leaf material. In Soil Organisms, J. Doebsen and van der Drift (Eds.) North Holland Publishing Co., Ansterdam 76-80.

Edwards,C.A and Lofty,J.R(1972)

Biology of earthworms Chapman and Hall Ltd. London

El.Duweini,A.K. and Ghabbour,S.I. (1965)

Population density and biomass of earthworms in different types of Egyptian soils. F. appl.Ecol.2, 271-87.

Evans, A.C.(1948).

Some effects of earthworms on soil structure. Ann. appl. Biol. 35, 1-13.

Evans, A.C and Guild , W.J. Mc.L.(1947).

Studies on the relationships between earthworms and soil fertility. i. Biological studies in the field Ann. appl.Boil. 307-30.

Evans, A.C.and Guild, W.J. Mc.L.(1948)

Studies on the relationships betweem earthworms and soil fertility. IV On the life cycles of some British Lumbricidae Ann. Biol 35(4) 471-84.

Finck, A. (1952).

Ecological and pedological studies on the effects of earthworms on soil fertility, Z.Pfl Ernahr. Ding 58, 120-145.

Fragoso, C. (1985).

Ecologia general de las Lombrices terrestres de la region Boca del chajul, Selva Lacandona, Ph.D Thesis, UNAM, Mexico.

Franz,H. and Leitenberger L. (1948).

Biological-chemical investigation into the formation of humus through soil animals Ost. Zool.Z.1(5) 498-578

Gates,G.E. (1959)

Bull.Mus. comp.Zool, Harv 121,220-61

Gaur, A.C, Neelakantan, S., Dargan, K.S, (1984).

Organic manures, Indian Council of Agricultural Research, New Delhi, 44

Guerro, R.D. (1981).

The culture and use of Perionyx excavatus as a protein resource in Philippines Proceedings of the Darwin Centenary Symposium, Grange-over Sands, Cumbria, 22

Gerard, B.M. (1967).

Factors affecting earthworms in pastures, Journal Anim. Ecol. 36:235-252.

Gersch.M. (1954).

Effect of Carcinogenic hydrocarbons on the skin of earthworms Naturwissenschaften, 41,337.

Graff,O. (1953)

Investigations in soil zoology with special reference to the terricole Oligochaeta Z. Pflirnahr Ding 61, 72-7.

Graff,O. (1974)

Gewinnung von Biomasse aus Abfallstoffen durch Kultur des Kompostregenwurms Eisenia foetida (Savigny 1826). Landb Forsch Volkenrode 24, 137-142.

Guild, W.J. Mc.L. (1952a)

Variation in earthworm numbers within field populations F.Anim. Ecology 21(2) 169.

Guild, W.J. Mc.L. (1952b)

The Lumbricide in upland areas 11. Population variation on hill pasture. Ann.Mag.nat. Hist.12(5).286-92

Guild, W.J. Mc.L, (1955)

Earthworms and soil structure In: Soil Zoology, D.K. Mc.E. Kevan (Ed.) Butterworths, London pp 83-98.

Gupta, O.P. (1979).

Aquatic weeds : Their menoce and control, Today and Tomorrow's publishers, New Delhi, 172-175.

Hamblyn, C.J., and Dingwall, A.R., (1945).

Earthworms *N.Z. Fl. Agric* 71, 55-8.

Hartenstein, R., Neuhauser, E.F., and Kaplan, D.L. (1979).

Reproductive potential of the earthworm Eisenia foetida. Oecologia (Berl), 43, 329-340.

Hartenstein, R. (1981).

Potential use of earthworms as a solution to sludge management. Water Pollution Control. 638-643.

Hasenbein,G.(1951)

A pregnancy test on earthworms Arch. Gynakol. 181, 5-28.

Heymons, R. (1923).

The influence of earthworms on the structure and yield of soils, Z. Pflanz. Dung, 2, 97-129.

Hinrichs, R.A. (1992)

Energy Saunder College Publishing

Hogben, L. and Kirk, R.L. (1944)

Body temperature of worms in moist and dry air. Proc. Roy.Soc. Lond. 132b, (868) 239-52.

Hopp, H. (1947)

The ecology of earthworms in cropland. Soil Sci. Soc.Amer. Proceedings 12, 503-7

Hopp, H. and Slater C.S. (1949)

The effect of earthworms on the productivity of agricultural soil, **Journal of** Agriculture Research, 78, 325-339.

Howard, A. ,(1933).

The waste products of Agriculture : their utilization as humus, Journal of Royal Society of Art 82 : 84-120. Indian Council of Agricultural Research. New Delhi 44.

Ismail, S.A., Seshadari, C.V., Jeiji Bai, N., and Suriyakumar, C.R. Shri, A.M.M. Muraugappa Chettiar Research Centre, Photo - (1993).

Synthesis and Energy Division, Tharamani. Chennai, India, Composting through earthworms, monograph series on the Engineering of photosynthetic systems, vol.35.

Ismail, S.A. (1996)

Vermitech (Vermicompost and Vermiwash) Institute of Research in Soil Biology and Biotechnology, New College, Chennai.

Ismail, S.A., (1997).

Vermicology : The Biology of Earthworms Orient Longman 92 pages.

Jadhav M.J., and Babar, S.S,. (1990).

Preliminary observation on production of compost from bagasse, pressmud and spentwash, Agricultural paper of the fortieth Annual convention of the Deccan Sugar Technologists Association. Pune, India, Deccan Sugar Technologists Association.153-160.

Johnstone - Wallace, D.B. (1937).

The influence of wild white clover on the seasonal production and chemical composition of pasture herbage and upon soil temperatures. Soil moistures and crosion control, 4th Int. grassl. Congr. Rep. 188-96.

Kahsnity, H.G. (1992).

Investigations on the influence of earthworms on soil and plant. *Bot. Arch* 1 315-51.

Kaplan, D.L., Hartenstein, R., Neuhauser, E.F. and Malerki, M.R.U. (1980)

Physiochemical requirements in the environment of the earthworm, Eisenin fetida, Soil Biology and Biochemistry 12: 347-352.

Keller, C. (1983).

The animal world in Agriculture, Leipzig.

Keup, E. (1913).

Feeding and activity of earthworms in relation to agriculture, Mitt cleutsch. landw. Ges, 28, 538-542.

Kimura, Y,. (1992).

Method and apparatus for producing organic fertiliser with the use of Nitrogen Bacillus, United States patent US5, 093, 262, 21PP.

Kollmannsperger, F. (1955).

Can earthworms be utilised and are they poisonous? Decheniana 105/106, 189-193.

Lalitha, R. (1997)

Vermicompost as carrier for Biofertilizers. Vermitech Worm Powered Technology issued on the occasion of the awareness-cum-training programme on Vermitech in Organic Farming IRSBB Special Publication.

Land,R. (1931).

Real and apparent crumb structure and tilth, Forstwiss. Cbl, 53, 309-324, 351-367, 393-403.

Lau DCW, Wu M M W (1987).

Manual composting as an option for utilisation and management of animal waste. Resource and conservation 13 145 - 156.

Lavelle, P. (1978).

Les Vers de terre de la savane de Lamto : Peuplements, populations et fonctions dans l'ecosysteme. Doctoral Thesis, Univ. Paris, VI Publ. lab Zool, EMS12.

Lavelle, P. (1984).

The soil system in the humid tropics. Biol. Int. 9:2-17

Lavelle, P. (1988)

Earthworm activities and the soil system. Biol. Fertil. Soils. 6 237-251.

Lavelle, P. Sow. B, Schaefer, R. (1980).

The geophagous earthworm community in the Lamto Savanna: Niche part timing utilization of soil nutritive resources, In: Dindahd (Ed), Syracuse, Washington DC, 653-672.

Lavelle, P and Meyer J.A. (1983).

Allez-les-Vers, a simulation model of dynamics and effect on soil of populations of Millsonia anomala, In: Labrun Ph, Andre, A.M, de Medts A, Gregoire - Wibo (Wanthy G (Eds), New trends in soil biology—Dieu Brichart, Louvain-la-Neuve, 503-519.

Lavelle, P., Zaidi, Z., and Schaefer, R. (1983).

Interaction between earthworms, soil organic matter and microflora in an African savanna soil, In: Lebrun Ph, Andre AM, de Medts A, Gregoire Wib C, Wauthy G (eds) New trends in soil biology, Dieu Brichart, Louvain-la, Neuve, 253-259.

Laverack (1963).

The physiology of earthworms, Pergamon Press, Oxford.

Lee, K,E. (1959)

A key for the identification of New Zealand earthworms. Tuatara, 8(1) 13-60.

Lee, K.E (1985).

Earthworms: The ecology and relationships with soils and land use, Academic Press, and Anderson J.M. (1979): Decompostion in terrestrial ecosystems, Studies in ecology, Black well, Oxford, vol. 5.

Lindquist, B. (1941).

Investigations on the significance of some Scandinavian earthworms in decompostion of leaf litter and the structure of mull soil, Svenska Skog Foren. Tidokr, 39, 179-242.

Lofs - Holmin A, (1986).

Processing of municipal sludges through earthworms (Dentrobaena veneta) Swedish Journal of Agricultural Research 16: 67 - 71.

Lunt, H.A. and Jacobson, G.M. (1944).

The chemical composition of earthworm costs, Soil Science, 58, 367-375.

Madge, D.S. (1966)

How leaf litter disappears. New Scientist 32, 113-15.

Madge,D.S.(1969)

Field and laboratory studies on the activities of two species of trophical earthworms. Pedobiologia 9, 188-214.

Marshall, V.G. (1972).

Effects of soil arthropods and earthworms on the growth of Black spruce. Proc 4th Int. Congr. Soil Zoll.

Martin, A., Cortez, J., Barois, I. and Lavella, P. (1987).

Les mucus de Ver de terre moteus de leurs interactions avec la microflore, Rev.Ecol.Biol.Sol. 24:549-558.

Mathur, B.S., Sarkar, A.K., Mishra, B (1980).

Release of Nitrogen and Phosphorous from compost charged with rock phosphate Journal of the Indian society of soil science 28 : 206 - 212.

Michaelsen, W.(1910)

Die Oligochatenfauna der vorderindischceylonischen Region. Abh. Natural. Hamburg 19.

Michon, J. (1954)

Influence de l'isolement a parter de la maturite sexuelle sur la biologic des Lumbricidea C.R. hebd. seanc. Acad. Sci., Paris, 238, 2457-8.

National Academy of Sciences (1976)

Integrated Systems In : Making Aquatic Weeds Useful : Some Perspectives for Developing Countries, NAS, Washington DC 115-125

Needham, A.E. (1957).

Components of nitrogenous excreta in the earthworms Lumbricus terrestris and Eisenia foetida, Journal exp.Biol, 34(4), 425-446.

National Environmental Engineering Research Institute Nagpur India.

Shanti N.R. Bhoyar, R.V and Bhide, A.D.

Nye, P.H. (1955).

Some soil farming processes in the humid tropics, The action of soil fauna, Journal of Soil Science, 6, 73-83.

O'Brien, B.J. and Stout. J.D 1978

Movement and turnover of soil organic matter as indicated by Carbon isotope measurements. Soil Biology and Biochemistry, 10, 309-317.

Olsen,H.W. (1928)

The earthworms of Ohio, Ohio biol. surv. Bull.17, 47-90.

Omodeo, P. (1958)

La reserve naturelle integrale d Mont Nomba. I. Oligochaetes, mem, Inst. fr. Afr. noire, 53, 9-10.

Outerbridge, T. (1991)

The Big Backyard Composting strategies in N.Y. The Ecologist 24(3)

Parr J.F. 1981,

Management of organic recycling. Project field document.No.16 Rome, Italy : Food and Agriculture Organization.

Parton, W.J., Anderson, D.W., Cole, C.V. and Stewart, J.W.B (1984).

Simulation of soil organic matter fermation and mineralization in semiarid agroecosystems, In: Lowrance R (Ed) Nutrient cycling in agricultural ecosystems, Univ. Georgia, Spec. Publ 23:533-550.

Peavy, H.S. Rowe; D.R and George Tchobanoglous (1985)

Environmental Engineering McGraw-Hill International Editions Civil Engineering Series.

Piearce, T.G. (1978)

Gut contents of some lumbricide earthworms. Pedobiologia, 18, 153-157.

Pineda, A. and Hernandez, A.H. (1983).

Effects de la temperture sobre el crecimiento consumo de tierray fecundidad de la lombriz de tieara Pontoscolex corethrurus Muller, Thesis, Univ, Natle, Maxico

Ponomareva, S.I. (1948).

The rate of formation of calcite by earthworms in the soil, Dokl. Akad. Nauk, 61, 505-507.

Ponomareva, S.I. (1950).

The role of earthworm in the creation of a stable structure in ley rotations, Pochvovednie, 476-486.

Powers, W.L. and Bollen, W.B (1935).

The chemical and biological nature of certain forest soils, Soil Science, 40, 321-329.

Puh, P.C. (1941).

Beneficial influence of earthworms on some chemical properties of the soil, Sci.Soc.China, Biol.Lab.Contrib., Zool. Scr, 15, 147-155.

Rafidison, Z (1982).

Role de la fauna dans l' humification: Transformations de feuilles de Letre par un ver anecique Nicodrilus velox, PhD Thesis, Univ. Naney

Ramasamy E.V. and Abbasi S.A. (2000)

High-solids anaerobic digestion for the recovery of energy and manure from municipal solid waste (MSW), Environmental Technology (in press)

RAPA , (1988).

Bio and organic fertilizers prospects and progress in Asia Bull No: 10:50 Bangkok : Regional office for Asia and Pacific, food and agriculture organization.

Reinecke, A.J., Hayes J.P. and Cilliers. S.C. (1991)

Protein quality of three different species of earthworms in S. Afr. Journal of Animal Science 21(2) 99-103.

Rhee, J.A. Van (1965).

Earthworm activity and plant growth in artificial cultures. Pl. and soil, 22, 45-8.

Richards, J.G. (1955).

Earthworms (recent research work) *N.Z. Jl. Agric* 91, 559.

Ribaudcourt, E. and Combault, A. (1907).

The role of earthworm in agriculture, Bull. Soc. for Belg.

Robertson, J.D. (1936).

The function of the calciferous glands of earthworms, Journal exp.Biol., 13, 279-297.

Rodale, J.I,.(1960).

The complete Book of Composting USA Rodale Books, Inc.

Russell, E.J. (1910).

The effect of earthworms on soil productiveness, Journal of Agriculture Science, 3, 246-257.

Sabine, J.R. (1978).

The nutritive value of earthworm meal, In: Utilization of soil organisms in sludge management, (Ed) R.Hartenstein, 122-130

Salisbury, E.J. (1923).

The influence of earthworms on soil reaction and the stratification of undisturbed soils, Journal Linn. Soc, 46, 415-425.

Satchell, J.E. (1955)

Some aspects of earthworm ecology Soil Zoology, D.K. Mc.E.Kevan (Ed) Butterworths, London, pp 180-201

Satchell, J.E. (1963)

Nitrogen turnover by a *woodland population of Lumbricus terrestris*. In Soil Organisms, J. Doeksen and J. Van der Drift (Eds) North Holland Publishing Co., Amsterdam 60-66.

Satchell, J.E. (1967).

Earthworms, In: Burges A, Raw F (Eds) Soil biology, Academic Press, London, New York, 259-322.

Seenappa. S.N. and Kale R.D. (1995)

Efficiency of earthworm Eudrilus eugeniae in converting the solid waste from Aromatic oil extracting units into vermicomposting Journal IAEM 22, 267-269.

Seenappa. C., Jagannatha Row C.B., (1995)

Conversion of distillery waste into organic manure using earthworm Ecudrilus eugeniae kinb. In: Proceedings of third international conference on Appropriate waste management technologies for developing countries, NEERI, Nagpur, India 1165-1170

Senapati B.K and Dash M.C (1982)

Earthworm as waste conditioner. Industrial Eng. J (Energy management issue) XI (2): 53-57

Senapati, B.K and Dash M.C (1984)

Functional role of earthworms in the decomposer subsystem. Tropical ecology 25, No.1 52-71

Senapathi, B.K. (1992)

Vermitechnology: *An Option for Recycling of cellulosic waste in India.* New Trends in Biotechnology. (Eds). N.S. Subba Rao, C. Balagopalan, S.V. Ramakrishna. Publ. Oxford & IBH, New Delhi, India, 347-358.

Senapati, B.K. (1993)

Vermitechnology in Integrated Waste Biomass Management; Concepts, Prospects and Problems. Biogas Slurry Utilization.

Sharma N and Madan M (1983).

Earthworms for soil health and pollution control, Journal of Scientific and Industrial Research, Vol 42, 575-583.

Singh, S,. Mishra, M.M,. Goyal, S,. Kapoor, K.K,(1992).

*Preparation of nitrogen and phosphorous enriched compost and its effect on wheat (Triticum destivum).*Indian Journal of Agricultural Sciences 62, 810-14.

Svendsen, J.A. (1955).

Earthworm population studies a comparison of sampling methods. Nature Lord, 175, 864.

Stephenson, J.(1930)

The Oligochaeta. Oxford University Press. 978 pp.

Stockdill, S.M.J. (1959).

Earthworms improve pasture growth N.Z.J. Agric 98, 227-33.

Stockli, A. (1928).

Studies on the influence of earthworms on the soil condition, Land W.Jb. Schweiz, 42, 5-121.

Stockli, A. (1949).

The influence of microflora and fauna on soil conditions, Z.Pfl Ernahr. Dung, 45, 41-53.

Stout, J.D. and Goh, K.M. (1980).

The use of radiocarbon to measure the effects of earthworms on soil development, Radiocarbon 22:892-896.

Stout, J.D., Goh, K.M. and Rafter, T.A. (1981).

Chemistry and turnover of naturally occuring resistant organic compounds in soil, In: Paul E.A, I add 1 N (Eds), Soil biochemistry, Dekker, New York, Vol.5, 73.

Svendsen, J.A. (1957a)

The distribution of Lumbricidae in an area of Pennine Moorland (Moor House, Nature Reserve) F.Animal Ecology 26(2) 409.

Svendsen, J.A. (1957b)

The behaviour of lumbricids under moorland conditions F. Anim. Eco.26(2) 423-39.

Swift,M.J. Heal, O.W. and Amderson, J.M. (1979)

Decomposition in Terrestrial Ecosystems. Blackwell, Oxford 372 pp

Tandon, HLS.(1994).

Fertilizers, Organic manures recyclable wastes and biofertilizers. Development and consultation organisation, New Delhi (India)

Toutain, F. (1981).

Les humus forestiers, Structures et modes de function rement, Rev. for Fr (Nancy) 33: 449-477

Van Gansen, P. (1962).

Structures et functions due tube degestif du lombricien Eisenia fetida, PhD thesis, Univ. Brussels.

Veeresh, G.K. (1984)

Prospects and Future of Earthworm utilization in India. Nat. Sem. on. Organic Waste Utilization and Vermicomposting.

Vimal, O.P and Talshilkar, s. (1982)

Recycling of Wastes in Agriculture. Looking ahead to 2000 A.D

Watson, M.R. and Smith, R.H. (1956).

The chemical composition of earthworm cuticle, Biochem. Journal 64(1), Proceedings biochem. Soc., 10.

Weisbach, W.W. (1962)

Regenwiirmer and Essbare Erde Boil. Jaarb.Dodonea. 30, 225-38.

Wilson D.C (1981)

Waste Management Planning, Evaluation, Technologies, Clarenndon Press Oxford.

Wittich, W. (1952).

Our present knowledge about humus and the new approach to solving the raw-humus problem in forests, Schr Reiha forstl.Fak Gottingen, 4, 1-106.

Yoshida, M abd Hoshu, H. (1978)

Nutritional value of earthworms for poultry feed Fpn. poult.Sci. 15, 308-311.

Zaidi, Z. (1985).

Recherches Sur les modalities de interdependence nutrits mannalle entre vers de terre et microflora dans la savane guinenne de Lamto, PhD thesis, Paris.

Zragherskii, A.J. (1957).

Dozydevye chervi kak fakter ploderodiya lesnykh pochv. Kiev. 135pp.

INDEX